Social Skills

How to Analyze People and Body Language Instantly, Handle Small Talk and Conversation as an Introvert, Improve Emotional Intelligence, and Learn Highly Effective Communication Tips

© **Copyright 2019**

All Rights Reserved. No part of this book may be reproduced in any form without permission in writing from the author. Reviewers may quote brief passages in reviews.

Disclaimer: No part of this publication may be reproduced or transmitted in any form or by any means, mechanical or electronic, including photocopying or recording, or by any information storage and retrieval system, or transmitted by email without permission in writing from the publisher.

While all attempts have been made to verify the information provided in this publication, neither the author nor the publisher assumes any responsibility for errors, omissions or contrary interpretations of the subject matter herein.

This book is for entertainment purposes only. The views expressed are those of the author alone, and should not be taken as expert instruction or commands. The reader is responsible for his or her own actions.

Adherence to all applicable laws and regulations, including international, federal, state and local laws governing professional licensing, business practices, advertising and all other aspects of doing business in the US, Canada, UK or any other jurisdiction is the sole responsibility of the purchaser or reader.

Neither the author nor the publisher assumes any responsibility or liability whatsoever on the behalf of the purchaser or reader of these materials. Any perceived slight of any individual or organization is purely unintentional.

Contents

INTRODUCTION 1
CHAPTER 1: HOW TO DEAL WITH SOCIAL ANXIETY 3
CHAPTER 2: THE IMPORTANCE OF SOCIAL SKILLS 8
CHAPTER 3: INTROVERT TRAITS 14
CHAPTER 4: GOALS 20
CHAPTER 5: ANALYZING PEOPLE 26
CHAPTER 6: BODY LANGUAGE 32
CHAPTER 7: FACE READING 38
CHAPTER 8: THE FOUR PERSONALITY TYPES 43
    CHOLERIC 44
    SANGUINE 45
    PHLEGMATIC 46
    MELANCHOLIC 47
CHAPTER 9: HOW TO DETECT A LIAR 49
CHAPTER 10: MAKE BODY LANGUAGE YOUR SUPERPOWER 55
CHAPTER 11: HANDLING SMALL TALK AS AN INTROVERT 61
    WHY IS SMALL TALK DIFFICULT AND DESIRABLE FOR INTROVERTS? 62
CHAPTER 12: INTROVERT PROBLEMS AND RELATIONSHIPS 67

CHAPTER 13: INTROVERT PROBLEMS IN AN OPEN WORKPLACE . 73

CHAPTER 14: INTROVERT PROBLEMS AT SOCIAL GATHERINGS, EVENTS, AND PARTIES 79

CHAPTER 15: EMOTIONAL INTELLIGENCE 84

  WHAT IS THE IMPORTANCE OF EMOTIONAL INTELLIGENCE, PARTICULARLY FOR YOU? 86

CHAPTER 16: PRACTICAL COMMUNICATION TIPS (ADDITIONAL TIPS) 90

CHAPTER 17: INSPIRING INDIVIDUALS 95

CONCLUSION 99

Introduction

There are many misconceptions about introverts, such as how they are seen to be antisocial, unfriendly, shy, reserved, lonely – the list could go on and on. However, what does not get mentioned nearly enough is that being an introvert or having introvert tendencies can be a real *asset*.

The following chapters will discuss the process of developing good social skills if you identify as an introvert and draw from relevant modern examples. Topics such as dealing with social anxiety, developing introvert traits into more sociable traits, body language, and learning how to interact with different types of people will also be explored.

As a whole, the book provides pertinent advice based on modern research and an overview of some reputable people and how they socialize. The process of communication is important, and this book will enable you to understand the basic concepts of effective communication. This way, it becomes possible to understand the different characteristics of different individuals, including how to identify a liar – and this will help you, the reader, be much more effective at social interactions.

It will also cover the most effective ways of handling oneself in a social gathering, as portraying a good image among several people is an important aspect of socialization.

After reading this informative book, if you identify as an introvert or harbor introvert tendencies, then you'll be able to overcome your fears and anxieties, and generally change the way you present yourself both in professional and social settings.

An important note to remember as you read along is that you are *not* alone and there is *nothing* wrong with you. The world is full of people who have the same communication 'hiccups', and just because you will go on to master some talking techniques does not mean that the essence of who you are will entirely change. You will still be *you* – just with more confidence!

Introverts are people who get their energy from spending time alone (which is more often than not a good thing!). Like a battery, you take the time to recharge before unplugging again and stepping back out to face and interact with a beautiful but also chaotic world.

Chapter 1: How to Deal with Social Anxiety

Social skills are, unfortunately, a necessity in everyday life, whether it is in a professional or social setting. Fear and anxiety are among the major factors that determine a person's social skills, and understanding the impact they have on each person is vital. Most people are unable to stand in front of a large crowd and address them because of stage fright, and this fear always has an impact on how a message is delivered. Similarly, when interacting among people either at a social gathering or professional setup, fear and anxiety have a major impact on how a person will interact with others. It is important for you to understand, though, that fear is all 'in the mind' – rest assured as it *is* possible to alleviate it permanently with the right practice.

For most people who are just like you, either identify as an introvert or have introvert tendencies, standing in front of a crowd is as daunting as facing a bear all alone in the middle of the wilderness. This fear is developed as a result of constantly avoiding the importance of developing interactive social skills, and anxiety is inflated as a result of the realization that social interactions can be difficult. However, *it is possible* to get past this through experiences such as repeatedly talking in front of large crowds, which eventually eliminates the fear associated with social interactions. The same goes for interactions that involve one-on-one discussions where understanding different aspects of social skills can make a tremendous difference.

In order to apply the concepts mentioned in this book, it is necessary for you, the reader, to set up a foundation that will enable you to understand the best ways of improving your social skills:

Understand that fear and anxiety are all in your head (yes – it's easier said than done!): The most important part of developing good social skills is having supreme confidence in yourself. Developing good social skills means that the people surrounding you must be able to understand and interact with you in a normal way. This can only be achieved if you're confident about what you say because this lends legitimacy to you. Confidence can be developed by perfecting the elements of the message being communicated such that when you are in front of people, you can speak uninterrupted and thus inspire confidence in others.

Have an open mind: It is extremely important to keep an open mind as this will enable you to be open to different ideas. Fear and anxiety are caused by different reasons for every person, and thus it is important to remain receptive to advice and be willing to try out new things. One reason why fear and anxiety manifest for so long is that we often fail to recognize other ways that we may combat these problems. Thus, the process of improving social skills will be dependent on you being receptive to new ideas that can be implemented to a positive effect. The ideas suggested in this book are generalized and cover a wide scope of character traits, and it is important to remain receptive to the different ways of handling your improvement of social skills.

What role do fear and anxiety play in the development of your social skills and interactions?

Limits constructive thinking: Your social skills become inhibited when you focus on the fear and anxiety consuming you. This means that there is not enough time to do constructive thinking and relay a decent conversation or speech. Stage fright is an excellent example of the manifestation of fear and anxiety, and it limits the way you think and present ideas. Therefore, fear and anxiety can negatively impact social interactions because you are unable to express yourself fully, which results in ineffective communication.

Prevents effective communication: Fear and anxiety result in quietness, meekness and even confusion when you are interacting with other people. Therefore, being overcome with fear will only result in no communication at all, and this impacts the ability of others to understand you. Good social skills cannot be enhanced when you only focus on the fear because that is simply all you're thinking about. You overcrowd your head with thoughts of what your colleagues must be thinking of you, your appearance and even the sound of your voice. Thus, it becomes practically impossible to achieve effective communication in such a situation.

Distracts the listeners: Fear and anxiety not only hampers your social skills and interactions but also distracts your listener(s) from what is important. Whether it is in a social gathering or a one-on-one situation, you are more likely to get attention for your ineffective communication and open display of fear than for the message you're trying to communicate. This is ineffective when an important message has to be passed along because the person(s) will be focused on the fear you are displaying. This is a major disadvantage as it prevents the development of social skills.

Limits how to make friends: Ineffective social skills of interaction are developed because you cannot communicate out of fear and anxiety. You will spend a large amount of time thinking about your weaknesses when interacting socially with others, thereby limiting your chances of making friends. You probably find it particularly difficult meeting new people and assessing their characters, meaning that you find it incredibly difficult to make friends. This is a big disadvantage of the fear and anxiety that characterizes you because you consequently are unable to interact properly. Making friends is a critical part of interacting socially, and the inability to do this is a major disadvantage because friendship can further be a rewarding gift for people. With friends also comes the opportunity to flourish and allow yourself actually to *be* yourself, as we often befriend those who have similar qualities, opinions, and outlooks as us. Thus, the result is a positive relationship.

Communication might not be taken seriously: As already mentioned, when fear overcomes you, it sometimes shows, and this can limit the communication process as it can easily make a message dismissible. The elements of effective communication involve eloquence and appropriate body language, particularly when something important must be communicated.

Inability to effect a presentation: In a professional setting or a social situation, the ability to properly effect a presentation is affected by fear and anxiety. Proper communication requires that you reach out to everyone regardless of their characters. However, fear limits this ability because you are more focused on yourself rather than on communication. It is necessary to consider the importance of confidence when conducting a presentation as it is the only effective way of interacting with others when communicating something important.

Limits communication opportunities in the future: Your ability to communicate and relay messages in the future gradually disappears because of your inability to interact with other people socially. Fear limits different opportunities that would otherwise be available because you cannot concentrate on anything else other than your pitfalls when you are communicating with others. Romantically, it is possible to lose a mate as a result of ineffective communication because some people do not like those who are anxious or fearful. It is important to get around the problem of fear to ensure communication opportunities still exist in the future as fear makes other people have a lower opinion of you. The fact remains that social anxiety is something that can be controlled and, eventually, eliminated by understanding the basic role that fear plays in the interaction process. When you discover the influence of anxiety and fear over your life, trust us – you will be in a better position to make good decisions regarding how you interact with other people.

The secret to developing good natural charisma and getting over anxiety is, alas, through experience – and practice! Although it might sound harsh, it's a "tough love" approach: you *must* set your mind to the possibility of getting over your introvert tendencies so that you can develop more interactive ones.

But don't worry – we're here to help remember!

Chapter 2: The Importance of Social Skills

Social skills describe the basic approach to communication within society. The definition encompasses both non-verbal and verbal forms of communication because both are an essential element of good social skills. People interact with one another and even work together as a result of exercising social skills, bringing people with common goals and backgrounds together. Social skills allow for broader interactions among people from various backgrounds, thereby enabling mutually beneficial relationships to be established in society.

Everybody in society, not just you, will benefit from mastering social skills because it results in a progressive benefit for everybody concerned. First, mastering social skills allows you to improve existing relationships and allows people to feel closer to each other. Good social skills emphasize the virtues of honesty and togetherness, and this encourages closeness among different people. It is easier for somebody to like a charismatic person more than they would like an ordinary person because the former can express greater social skills. The same goes for romantic relationships because it is possible to improve such relations as a result of excellent social skills that encourage open communication. It is easier for people to forge strong relationships with each other because of social skills as it allows for easier communication and encourages action.

As touched on, excellent communication skills coupled with a good way of expressing yourself is a sure-fire way of attracting new friends. It is easier to catch the eye of somebody you would otherwise never speak to if they happen to experience your improved social skills. Everybody likes an eloquent, outspoken individual, and this is critical in the process of communicating and interacting with others. Getting a message across can be the difference between success and failure, and thus if you understand and have mastered social skills, you will rarely be misquoted. This also applies for presentations and public speaking as you will no longer struggle to make your point in front of a crowd. You will communicate with several people as though they were your personal friends.

Most professionals have achieved success in advancing their careers as a result of the mastery of social skills. Understanding how to relate to the people around you is critical for success within a professional setup. This is because it is necessary not only to be a good team player but also a manager and judge of character that positions the company for success. Social skills enable you to conduct yourself appropriately and win over several friends who end up being a big help in advancing your career. Good social skills also allow for closer interactions with customers, and they are responsible for building up a business and allowing those involved to enjoy success.

You can also enjoy a better reputation as a result of having good social skills. This is because you endear yourself to people far better than somebody who does not have good social skills. For instance, presidents and other leaders who display excellent social skills both in public and in private can command the respect of several people. As a result, they can automatically have a good reputation among different communities as compared to a person who is unable to express themselves appropriately.

It is possible to be much happier with yourself as a result of mastering social skills as compared to the depression caused by being alone. Most introverts, naturally but unfortunately, ignore the possibility of increasing their social skills because they do not see the benefit of doing it – or rather, their fear, yet again, holds them back. They would rather keep to themselves and be as private as possible as compared to getting out there to interact with other people. This concern is usually brought about by the need to live a private life and keep away from other people; however, the fact remains that society can only progress when everybody works together. Thus, the common belief by introverts is that they do not need to interact with the rest of society; however, this has the damaging consequence of bringing depression and general unhappiness. Good social skills allow you to walk around feeling free and open, never obligated into specific action but with the freedom to make choices. Interacting with other people is an essential part of ensuring happiness among a community of people, and thus personal happiness should be a critical reason for anyone to master social skills.

Should you desire a wider audience for your business or any social reason, mastering social skills can make a tremendous difference. Even internet communication, such as posting tweets, is dependent on good social skills as it will determine the nature of communication between you and your audience. Good social skills will allow you to have a much larger audience because your communication is effective and desirable to a large number of people. This way, it is possible to communicate an important message as well as advertise for your business successfully.

Another critical benefit of good social skills is that they allow you to be accepted in different social groups and among various peers. The ability to communicate effectively without fear or anxiety endears you to many different people and grants you access to different opportunities. People who explore the world and get to see many different things can do so because they are not introverts (*lucky them, huh? – but hey, it can be you too!)*. Their mastery of social skills allows them to penetrate different social groups and see as much as possible. Acceptance of different peers can be possible by anybody with a mastery of social skills.

It is quite difficult to "make it" in society alone because we rely on each other one way or another. So, here are some vital points on how to help you with your introvert tendencies:

Match conversations with friends and diversify: Speak to a close friend or family member to improve your social skills. It is critical to get a trusted person's help because they will be honest and guide you through the process reasonably. There is also the need to be respectful of their opinions as there is a reason you have selected them to help you. Practicing forthcoming conversations, whether it is in front of a gala dinner or trying to get a date, will help as it will allow you to anticipate what is coming. Diversifying is also an important aspect of improving social skills because it is necessary to interact with people outside of your normal scope of friends or even culture. Learning the perspectives of life from somebody new is important in helping you to master social skills because it gives you a different perspective. People from different cultures interact in a manner that you might not be used to and the experience itself will bring new importance for you. Having a full mastery of social skills will open up your mind to new ideas and diverse ways of thinking.

Practice in front of the mirror: This is a necessary action because you have to instill confidence in yourself. Look at your face in the mirror, how you are dressed, and picture what other people will think about you. It is necessary to have confidence and use both facial expressions and other modes of body language as you communicate. The purpose of looking at yourself in the mirror is to understand that *there is nothing wrong with* you in your presentation and that you should have more confidence in yourself when you are in front of people.

Read more about social skills: There is a lot of content online that can inspire you to understand more about social skills and how to master them. This book offers a similar guide in these steps as practicing them enables you to build confidence in yourself progressively. Reading appropriate content online will provide you with the knowledge base you need to make better decisions and conduct yourself with more confidence with other people. Adding this knowledge is a necessity as it will allow you to be better placed to avoid your anxieties and develop greater confidence when facing a group of people. This also applies in a romantic situation.

Remember, practice makes perfect: It is important to keep up with practicing your social skills. After all, the experience of interacting with more and more people will be responsible for eliminating the fear and anxiety that holds you back. Continuously understanding that interacting with people gets easier day by day will help you develop strong social skills, and you *will* end up feeling confident in your interactions with others. Eventually, social interactions will stop being a problem because the constant practice has made you get used to being around different company. You will understand how to conduct yourself in different situations.

Get Inspiration from well-known figures: Reading up on people who are excellent at social skills is another way of preparing yourself to improve your social skills. Emulating a leader or celebrity figure will inspire more confidence and prompt you toward developing better social skills. You can emulate them because you feel comfortable with them and how they present themselves. This will be possible by copying some of the trends that you like, and it will allow you to understand that all the fear that's holding you back, causing you continuously (and annoyingly) to falter, is just in your head. An inspiring figure can be a useful guide on how best to conduct yourself in a social gathering to ensure that the people you are communicating with understand you well and even like you. Take, for example, a handsome actor; it is possible to emulate some of his or her actions and even statements when on a date. It can make such an encounter so romantic that it guarantees success within a short period.

Chapter 3: Introvert Traits

Are you actually an introvert?

This is an extremely important question to answer as it will determine the extent of your mastery of social skills. An introvert is a person who prefers to be alone in a surrounding that is calm. For the most part, they exert a lot of energy in the socialization process, but this is not to say that all introverts do not have social skills. A good example is a person who prefers to sit by his or herself on a balcony as a way of relaxing as compared to an extrovert who is more likely to go to a party in a similar situation.

There is nothing wrong with being an introvert; in fact, studies suggest that up to half the population in the United States are introverts. So, how do you know if you are an introvert?

Socialization: Attending parties constantly, engaging in frequent casual chats and seeking attention are activities most introverts would consider to be a chore. For them, socialization is done in a meaningful manner where the party attended will not be too loud and there will be less casual chats and more meaningful conversations. Being an extrovert seems a lot of work because you have to constantly deal with several people, leaving little time for deeper connections.

Networking is difficult: Most introverts do not find this effort appealing, and for them, networking is only done on an as-needed basis. The effort put into getting so many friends that you might only have one chat with them is undesirable for introverts. Thus, if you find that networking is a more difficult task than sitting down in a math class, then you could be an introvert. Social media is a particularly excellent platform for understanding the nature of extroverts. Most of them will post several personal pictures, spend lots of time engaging in conversation and having very large followings. In order to acquire this status, it is necessary to do a lot of networking to engage with as many people as possible to boost your popularity.

You have your own world: Do you constantly find yourself slipping into some fantasy world, maybe one you thought about or frequently dream about? Do you enjoy spending a lot of time in this fantasy world, and when you get out, do you usually feel recharged? Then you probably are an introvert. The fact that you have your own little world that you can slip into whenever you want to is a telling character trait that shows you are creative and spend a lot of time to yourself.

Spend a lot of time pursuing interests: Introverts are usually organized and systematic people to the extent that they always have goals they are pursuing. An introvert will set a target for themselves, and the task can range significantly in difficulty, but it is still a challenge. As time passes, the targeted task will eventually be completed, and this is probably going to take up a bulk of the time. These contrast the traits of an extrovert who is more institutionalized and the tasks they are likely to be pursuing will be professionally related. It is rare for an extrovert to spend much time with themselves as they are being swamped by friends constantly or online on social media.

You enjoy spending time alone: This is a commonly discussed trait about introverts that sometimes confuse others to think that they are anti-social. The simple fact remains that introverts prefer meaningful company, and when it is not there, they would rather be by themselves.

An extrovert society is alien: Most introverts find it very difficult to socialize and keep up with the world of an extrovert. The fact that there is almost no time to spend to themselves is worrying enough to see the world of an extrovert as very alien. An introvert needs lots of time to themselves as well as to conduct only a few meaningful conversations at a time. This is not possible for an extrovert, and it does make their world seem very different from that of an introvert. Generally, the latter would prefer to keep to themselves and not dwell among circles of people where they feel uncomfortable.

You work best alone: The pleasure of getting to do something by yourself is climaxed by the eventual success. An introvert would prefer not to blame somebody else but take on the challenge by themselves. Help can be solicited for a complicated, technical project, but the introvert will oversee the entire process with a precision that will end up impressing everyone around them. An extrovert would prefer to solicit as much help as possible and probably excel more working in a team. An introvert will do all the work and be very satisfied at the end of the day, a contrast to how extroverts work.

You spend much of time in your head: If you find that you daydream so much that sometimes it can distract you, you probably are an introvert. Spending a lot of time to yourself and enjoying it more than interacting with others shows a deeper nature of your intuition.

You have a close circle: Most introverts prefer having only a close clique of friends that they can trust and actually engage in conversation. Extroverts are outgoing people capable of having a conversation with people of multiple character traits at once and enjoy it. This is very different from most introverts who prefer spending quiet time with close friends that allows them to have philosophical discussions or talk about shared interests. This is perhaps a reason why introverts are termed as anti-social because they will not make friends with people they cannot have a discussion with, but will have very close bonds with people they share character traits with.

You are in constant search of knowledge: An introvert is never satisfied with what they know; they are constantly exploring to learn as much as possible. Most introverts like holidays that allow them to explore and interact with nature because it allows them to see the world and discover new things. In the same sense, they will spend lots of time buried in books trying to discover something new.

You stay out of the spotlight: Introverts prefer less attention; it is very difficult to find them at the core of disturbance. They would rather be away from prying eyes and let somebody else gain the reputation and recognition because the actual process of socializing is too tiring for them.

You are better at writing than speaking your thoughts: If you find yourself preferring the art of writing than speaking or performance, then you probably are an introvert. This is a discussion that several introverts usually have, particularly when comparing a movie to a book it is based on; most introverts usually prefer reading the book than watching the movie because it leaves greater room for imagination and enjoyment of the story. This is a different case as far as extroverts are concerned because some of them probably appreciate movies more than the books because a movie offers an opportunity to interact with others and getting to watch it in numbers.

You do not always have all the answers: Just because introverts are different from extroverts does not always make them smarter or more knowledgeable about things. They are just normal people but behave differently from the extroverts, and this has more to do with the brain than actual choices. There is a difference in the release of dopamine in the brain between introverts and extroverts, and this offers a solid account for the differences in character. Therefore, extroverts should not blame introverts and put them under pressure that they should know everything because they have an equal opportunity to get answers to the questions they have. This book will help you because it will show you that you should not be confused about whether you are an introvert.

Introverts do not hate people: It is commonly believed that just because an introvert does not like to socialize much, it means that they hate people. Introverts simply seek a meaningful connection each time they interact with others and end up establishing very close bonds with others. Therefore, introverts can easily be the best of friends.

Introverts do not necessarily want to be extroverts: Introverts are proud of themselves and how they conduct themselves. This is why they rely on their intuition to determine their behavior rather than on what the majority is doing. Thus, introverts do not necessarily want to be like everybody else and are pretty satisfied with themselves.

Introverts are not socially awkward: Introverts are surprisingly sociable people – only they keep a few friends and refrain from constantly chatting with people they do not know. This positive personality does not necessarily translate to introverts being socially awkward; they are the opposite of that.

Introverts are not rude: One might get the impression that an introvert is rude because they do not want to engage in conversation or even be at the same event. The simple fact remains that introverts are interesting people and are always looking to spend their time constructively; this does not mean that they are rude.

Introverts do not need to change: Introverts are very proud of themselves and sometimes might be forced to think about changing in order to fit into a social gathering. The simple fact remains that introverts are more likely to be accepted and liked by others if they maintain a specific character about them that comes to be associated with them.

Chapter 4: Goals

To improve your social skills, it is important first to set goals that are attainable. Consequently, you have to follow through with the set actions to achieve success in interacting better with others. This is necessary because failing to plan is planning to fail, and so it is necessary first to highlight areas of weakness that need immediate improvement and setting the right goals to achieve this.

Some might find this step a little too tiring because it will require a lot of preplanning and even reading, but it is necessary to understand its importance in improving social skills. Towards the end of this chapter, there will be a practical example set on how to set goals and successfully achieve them.

The following lists six reasons why setting goals are important in the process of improving your social skills:

Allows you to identify challenges beforehand: The importance of setting goals is so that you can understand the hurdles that face you before you have to interact with others. This is essential if you are going to get past your socialization problems, and it does not mean that you have to change your personality. The beauty about setting goals is that you can acknowledge the difficulties that face you before delving into them. This will allow you adequate time to be mentally prepared and is the first step towards understanding social skills.

Enables you to earn experience: The planning stage is important in any part of a strategy. Therefore, it is the perfect way for you to gain experience in some of the advantages and disadvantages of mastering social skills. It is rare that a plan goes exactly how you envisioned it, and this experience is useful for anybody learning social skills. This is because it is necessary to realize that there is no point in beating yourself down after one interaction because there are always several of them. Preparing for the next hurdle is more important, and each interaction should be treated as a learning experience.

Allows you to get a better understanding of your weaknesses: It becomes much easier to handle the specific weaknesses that inhibit you from interacting with others by first identifying those weaknesses. Everybody has different types of weaknesses, from hating long conversations, talking about certain topics and interacting with specific types of personalities. Identifying these weaknesses will enable a lot of time to be spent trying to understand how to tackle the problem and to practice. For instance, an introvert who does not like long conversations can find a smooth way of excusing themselves and slipping away.

Helps you practice: It is important to be able to recite your actions and prepare yourself on how to interact with others. This is the importance of setting goals as it enables you to have that critical mental preparation that will make all the difference. It is important to see yourself as a normal person and build up confidence, and this will readily be achieved by practicing beforehand. For example, it is possible to write out a short script and play it over to yourself or in your head. The importance of this is to give you a scope on the level of interactions you will have to engage in so that you can be prepared.

Helps you gain confidence: The process of setting goals will allow you to come to the task with the challenges that lay ahead and be able to implement a workable strategy. This is important because it will give you more confidence, an important trait you will need to have when mastering social skills. Nothing is intimidating about standing in front of a group of people and speaking to them, even if it is a romantic situation and you are trying to speak to the opposite sex. The fact remains that everybody likes somebody who can display confidence, and if you can, the chances are high that you will be liked. Setting goals beforehand, therefore, is critical to you attaining confidence and enabling you to understand the social skills you need.

Allows you to solicit the help of a friend: Setting goals will give you an opportunity to ask a close friend to help you master social skills. This is because there will be time for you to consult and practice together with your friend, allowing you to put into practice what you have already learned. This is a pretty effective technique as your friend can tell you how you are coming off and give you some tips on improvement. Setting goals enables you to foresee challenges that you would possibly encounter while interacting with others, and the help of a friend should make the entire process much easier for you.

Toby is an introvert, and he only has a few friends. However, he is still outgoing when you get the chance to interact with him, and he has recently been promoted to be the manager of his entire branch. He rarely attends parties, but not only will he have to attend the one celebrating his elevation to the position, but he will have to give a speech and interact endlessly with others. He only has a week to prepare, and his biggest concern is that he does not want to attend the party because he is not good at socializing. Therefore, he set himself the following goals and implemented them before the week was over:

Attend the neighborhood meeting: Being an introvert, it was the first time Toby was attending a neighborhood meeting. He did so to overcome his problem of having to engage in long conversations that were not particularly beneficial to him. However, by the end of the night, he was surprised by how invigorated he felt because he was able to speak to some of his neighbors whom he did not know but had some shared interests. He was able to overcome the problem of constantly fearing drawn-out conversations as they take up so much time and end up being very tiring. But in Toby's experience, the meeting was a success because it was preparing him for what was about to come.

Spending time in front of a mirror: Toby enhanced his understanding of facial expressions and body language by performing in front of a mirror. He recited a provisional speech and observed himself, gaining confidence and even deciding the best way of dressing. This was a good action because it was evident that the process was not too difficult to implement when trying to understand social skills. Spending time to himself to practice was important as it gave him a rough idea of how to conduct himself and even what to say.

Reading up about giving speeches: Toby found this topic to be surprisingly exciting because several good examples are presented online. Giving a speech is quite exciting, particularly when you have prepared for it, and Toby found that it was going to be easy for him to prepare the right words to say for the occasion. However, his main concern was stage fright because he was not used to speaking in front of several people at once. Even in the office, he was more of a man-manager because he liked working closely with each of his subordinates and carefully prepared them for their tasks. However, he found subtle advice by reading up on speeches about the best ways of overcoming stage fright, including focusing on the main elements of the communication but maintaining casual eye contact with the audience. The information turned out to be useful and reading up on it certainly gave him more confidence to prepare himself for the upcoming banquet.

Watched old Churchill tapes: Toby ended up spending an entire night watching old Winston Churchill tapes and spending time, in particular, watching how he gave speeches. He found the experience to be so intriguing that he was unable to sleep that night, but he did enjoy how Churchill delivered his message in the past. He watched everything about the great leader, coming to appreciate the importance of mastering language in communication, as well as the role that confidence played. His confidence was boosted tremendously after watching the tapes, and he started to think differently about how to overcome his socialization problems.

Practiced with his wife: Practicing with his wife turned out to be equally useful because he was able to get good advice on how to change some of his actions. His wife played the perfect role of an extrovert, putting Toby under pressure at different instances in order to help him get used to the day he was about to experience. Toby was able to identify further weaknesses in himself as his wife played the role of an extrovert, and this was crucial in helping him prepare how to conduct himself.

Setting these goals in advance turned out to be an excellent idea for Toby. The day turned out to be a good one for him because the practice that he was able to do throughout the week enabled him to socialize very well. He ended up having a lot of fun and endeared himself to his subordinates. After that day, he was already looking forward to his new role and interacting more with the employees at the organization. Understanding social skills requires goals to be set so that the process can be streamlined for success.

The example above is not to say that introverts can master social skills within a week. For most people, it will take varying amounts of time to understand basic social skills that allow them to spend extended amounts of time with extroverts. The fact remains that introverts will always be interested in and look forward to spending time with themselves, but it is also important to find a perfect balance that allows them to spend time with the people around them. Mastering the social skills necessary to be considered as "one of us" among a group of extroverts will take time and will require much practice. The importance of setting goals can make a significant difference in the mastery of social skills.

Chapter 5: Analyzing People

Analyzing people is a very important part of mastering social skills. The process of analyzing people gives you a better perspective on their character, behavior, and preferences. This is important to understand both in a professional setting and a social one because it enables you to tailor your interactions to each person. Everybody likes to feel special, so treating them in their own unique way is an excellent way of getting them to like you while you enhance your social skills. There are many reasons to analyze people:

To avoid surprises: Analyzing people will enable you to avoid compromising situations because you will be in a position to understand their preferences. You will not make mistakes ordinarily attributed to somebody who does not know how to deal with certain character traits. For example, it will be possible to avoid a scenario where you make a joke about a specific profession when it turns out the same people you are joking with happen to be in that profession! Analyzing people will give you tell-tale signs of who they are, and you will be in a better position to interact with them.

To judge character better: If you are going to interact with people successfully, it is important to judge their character to understand the type of conversation you will have with them. This is the reason for conducting analysis on people because it sheds a little light into who they really are and their motivations. This allows you to be more efficient with your decision making when interacting with such characters, and it becomes possible to know what to avoid when interacting with them. Judging character is a good way of better understanding a person and being in a position to interact well with them.

To prepare for interaction and avoid mistakes: Analyzing people gives you an opportunity to mentally prepare yourself on how to interact and what to say to them. It provides an opportunity to mull over appropriate subjects of conversation that will keep both parties interested, and it also highlights the best way of presenting yourself. This way it becomes possible to avoid common mistakes involved with social etiquette, and it limits the number of embarrassing moments for you. Analyzing people beforehand gives you the chance to ensure your interaction is a total success.

To better understand the context of interaction: The process of analyzing people within a certain context provides a better understanding of the interaction and how to conduct yourself. This is because it will provide information on the type of people in the social gathering. There will be a better understanding of the general crowd and the reasons for meeting up, thereby allowing you to behave in a specific way and get a better understanding of social skills.

There are a number of ways in which to analyze people. Below is a general guide on how you can achieve this:

Pay attention to posture: One of the subtlest ways of analyzing people is noticing how they position themselves. Different body postures are indicative of different moods that the person is experiencing, and this will be useful in understanding how to approach the person and what topics of conversation are most suitable. If a person's body posture is slumping, it is indicative of sadness and thus will be inappropriate to approach them and discuss an upcoming funeral.

Notice their appearance: The immediate appearance of a person speaks volumes about who they are and what they like. A good, positive appearance featuring good dressing and a generally happy posture means that the person is in a good mood and probably would be up for a conversation. The appearance of a person is one of the most direct forms of communication, and when generally looking at a crowd, it can dictate the type of people as well as their motives. A poor appearance discourages much interaction, and such people might not be the best to hang around with. It is possible to make important social decisions based on how the person is dressed.

Body Language: This describes the general body movements of a person and can play an important role in determining how you interact with them. For example, crossed arms and legs when sitting down can indicate the person is in a serious mood and does not have the time for jokes. Lip biting can suggest somebody who is nervous or agitated while the way somebody is leaning can be indicative of the people they like and those they would rather stay away from. Hiding the hands is another subtle form of body language that is indicative of someone's secretive nature.

Facial Expressions: Facial expressions are also an important way of analyzing other people in a social setting. A clenched jaw or teeth is indicative of somebody who is not at ease, and thus interacting with them should be done carefully. A crow's feet smile is indicative of somebody who is happy, and thus engaging in a merry conversation would not be off. A person with pursed lips is indicative of bitterness or even anger, and a person with deep frown lines is equally not happy or stressed. Thus, understanding these facial expressions is instrumental in analyzing people and forms an excellent basis for mastering social skills.

The tone of somebody's voice or even laughter: A low-pitched voice or laughter is indicative of somebody who is more relaxed and at ease. It will be best to introduce simple topics and chat belatedly with such a person in a social setting. A high-pitched voice or laughter, however, can be indicative of more than a single emotion; an agitated, angry person is likely to speak in a high-pitched voice, but somebody laughing equally loudly would be indicative that they are in a very good mood.

Pay more attention to a handshake: A simple handshake can be the basis for analyzing somebody because it can speak volumes about their state of mind and their mood. From a handshake, it is possible to tell whether you will be engaging with somebody further in conversation. Aggressive handshakes might be indicative of a loud and brash personality, a typical characteristic of extroverts. It might be simple enough to have a few words with such a person and move on because interacting with them might prove tiresome. However, a gentler handshake might speak of the personality of the person, and it might be easier to have a conversation with such a person in a social setting.

Watch their Eyes: It is possible to learn a lot about somebody simply by watching their eyes and monitoring how they observe everybody else. Somebody whose eyes are constantly darting all over the place might be indicative of a nervous person. It is likely that the person is also an introvert and is uncomfortable with being in such a setting. A person with a fixed facial expression with eyes trained on one place even if they are alone can be indicative of sadness or calmness.

Follow your intuition: You should analyze a situation for yourself by looking at everybody and remembering the aspects of social skills you have already mastered. You should always follow your gut feeling when making a decision because it is surprising how important a role intuition plays in the decision-making process. Having confidence in yourself will enable you to analyze people without much effort, and this will be a big plus when interacting with them. It enables you to develop a special mastery of judging character and understanding the behaviors of others even before you fully interact with them.

There are many factors for you to consider when you successfully analyze people in order to improve your social skills:

Improves communication: One critical benefit of understanding how to analyze people is that it makes the communication process more efficient. It becomes easier for you to make decisions based on your knowledge of the character and behavior of the people. Communication becomes simple enough because you can identify a single way of spreading a message to other people in the most appropriate manner possible. Analyzing people has the advantage of being able to speak to them comfortably.

Reduces chances of offending others: Understanding how people behave and interact with one another eliminates the chances of offending them when interacting with them. For instance, if you are speaking to a group of health professionals, it might be inappropriate to suddenly start talking about how healthcare has worsened over the years as they believe themselves to be dedicated professionals. Analyzing people beforehand has the benefit of helping you avoid the small offenses and being in a position to make appropriate decisions based on what you already know. This way, interacting with them becomes much easier.

Offers an opportunity to make friends: It is possible to understand the characters of different people as a result of analyzing them, and it makes it better to know whom to make friends with. Analyzing people will reveal basic facts about them, and this puts you in a better position to make judgments about their traits and whether you can spend time with them. You will be able to get information about them prior to actually interacting with them, and this can show you whether you would be interested in befriending them and furthering your friendship with them.

Allows efficient interaction with others: Analyzing other people will reduce the chances of you making mistakes when interacting with people because you have a better understanding of their preferences. It becomes much easier to be in a social setting where you will interact with different character traits, and it allows you to display your social skills to some of the people. Mastery of social skills will be dependent on your ability to understand the people around you because they make up the society in which you live in. As a result, the socialization process becomes much easier, and being nervous around other people slowly becomes a rarity.

Chapter 6: Body Language

Body language as a term describes the communication that somebody makes by using a part of their body to indicate their emotional state, to point out something, or to dismiss something. This is one of the oldest forms of communication and remains an important part of developing social skills because it helps to analyze people. Body language is a subtle way of communicating because it is difficult to misinterpret what is being communicated to another party. The clarity of body language makes it an assured way of understanding other people because how they behave with their bodies communicates volumes about them.

It is important to read body language in the process of mastering social skills because it will form the basis for your interactions with other people. The communication that you will get from their bodies will provide you with ample data to make decisions on their characters and behaviors. Understanding each person around us to the maximum is probably impossible because it would take up a significant amount of time. However, understanding the basic aspects of a person's character will make it easier for you to interact with them because you will know what to talk about and avoid what offends them.

The other advantage of understanding body language is that it enables one to be efficient in their interactions because they have a basic understanding of other people. Body language is an important form of non-verbal communication that, if understood, makes interacting with other people very simple. There is no need to bother interacting with a person who is letting off a negative vibe the whole evening; it is better to interact with the person on the dance floor the whole night because he or she is energetic and likely to be available for a good conversation.

There are many important forms of body language that you need to understand in order to know how to apply them in basic social situations. The following body language techniques are the basic forms of expression that people utilize whether consciously or unconsciously. They form the basis of understanding the character and state of mind of a person in that instance, and this makes it easier to interact with them. Every form of body language is a communication attempt by a person, and it is important in understanding social skills:

Head held in the hands: When you come across somebody in this posture, their body language easily suggests one option: sadness. Somebody who is literally hiding their face in their hands shows a great level of sorrow, and it would probably be best to console the person or let them be. This is an obvious body language communication, and it does not leave much to the imagination because the sadness of the person is obvious. It would probably be best not to crack jokes with them but try to come to terms with their somber mood.

Nose rubbing: Somebody who is constantly rubbing their nose probably knows something you do not or is very excited. For example, if you happen to be having a conversation with somebody who is constantly displaying this body language, he or she is probably excited about knowing something you do not know. It might be useful to engage them further in conversation to understand what they know, and it is also important to keep it respectful. Monitoring such body language expressions helps to understand the intentions of a person, particularly in a social context, and is a significant step towards mastering social skills.

Fidgeting: If someone is constantly fidgeting, it is highly likely that they are nervous about something and would not be willing to discuss it further. It is important to take note of such expressions as it helps in understanding what somebody is thinking and thus sets the grounds for interaction. A fidgety person will be at ease and will also speak with a lot of nervousness, making it difficult to understand them. Therefore, the best approach is to let them be or, if you have to speak to them, keep in mind that they are nervous.

Leaning at a distance: This is another important form of body language that indicates the likes and dislikes of somebody. If you come across somebody who is leaning close to somebody else or a group of people, this is indicative of his or her likeness for them. They are likely to be close friends, and people always lean close to the people they trust the most. However, leaning away from people would be indicative of a sense of mistrust, and if you walk into such a situation, you could be walking into a tense scenario. Therefore, how somebody positions themselves in a social gathering speaks volumes about their character.

Locked Ankles: When somebody has their ankles locked, it is indicative that they would rather not be disturbed or they have information they are not willing to share. Just like the gesture, locked ankles signify the withdrawal of the person because he or she is not that interested in interacting. It would be better to limit your interaction with such a person because they are not openly receptive. If you have to interact with them, however, keep it short because the person would only be interested in speaking if the matter was of absolute importance.

Restlessness: General restlessness speaks for itself because it is an indicator as to how comfortable a person is. Somebody who is constantly pacing up and down, unable to remain in one place at a time, is indicative of a nervous or agitated person. Such a person is likely to have their emotions running high, and so interaction should be minimized because it would not be possible to determine how successful one would be in interacting. Reading such signs will enable you to know exactly the sort of people to speak to, keeping in mind that restlessness shows that somebody is highly emotionally charged.

Active: An active body language indicates the eagerness of somebody to engage in an activity and might be an appropriate person to interact with. An active person will dance around, speak to several people and generally try to be outgoing in a social gathering. Such a person is likely to be in good spirits and should be easy to approach as they are in an openly interactive mood. It would be interesting to test your social skills with somebody resembling these character traits because they are openly receptive to interacting with almost anyone.

Arms crossed over chest: This is indicative of somebody who is in a serious mood and would prefer to minimize jokes and engage in constructive conversation. This body posture is a signature appearance for any child who ever made their parents cross and had to answer to them. Generally, interacting with such a person will involve a serious conversation where your social skills will be put to the test. It is important to remain calm and patient when interacting with such a person or else you will draw their retribution. Understanding the best approach to speaking to such a person will be a tremendous help in your quest to master social skills.

Drumming Fingers: Somebody who is displaying this body language is probably nervous and would like to minimize interactions. The drumming of the fingers means that the person has a lot on their mind, and unless you are a close confidant, they would not be willing to divulge this information. If you are on a date and they are constantly drumming their fingers, you might want to get into it a little more. Dates can be nerve-wracking sometimes, and talking about it with the opposite sex might create the light mood necessary for the interaction.

Nail biting: Another sign of nervousness is when somebody constantly has his or her fingers in their mouth. Most people bite their nails in an apparent distraction to their thoughts, but in reality, they think about it more when they are biting their nails. This is a classic type of body language, and it might be wise to approach such a person carefully – unless you know what is making them nervous. Interacting with such a person will involve a hushed, gentle conversation but it is unlikely to last very long unless they are willing to share the cause of their troubles.

Rubbing the hands: This is a body language expression that shows anticipation and excitement over something to come. Somebody who is constantly rubbing their hands probably has something interesting to say because they are openly showing their anticipation. Interacting with such a person would be interesting because they would be concealing the main aspects of their message while at the same time talking excitedly. Interacting with such a person would be a good experience for mastering social skills because it will involve you analyzing the person and determining whether he or she is being honest or not. This forms a basis for most decisions when making new friends.

Head tilted: This is indicative of somebody who is bored or sad, and thus will warrant a different approach when interacting with them. Somebody who is bored is very likely to tilt their head and stare nonchalantly into the distance probably deep in thought. They will not speak much, and approaching them might not change the situation much because they will not be looking to have a conversation. A sad person also tilts their head, and they will also not have much to say because some sorrow will be consuming them at that moment.

Placing the tips of the fingers together: Some people usually focus on touching just the index fingers, others choose to do this with all the fingers. Either way, it is an expression of power an intelligence over the audience of the person involved. Touching fingers together shows some level of superiority, and it might be useful first to know the person before interacting with them. Somebody who displays this body language is more likely to have something to say and so listening and talking less might be the best interaction in this case. A person with this personality will have a lot to teach you in terms of social interactions, and it will enable you to master the basics of social skills.

The process of analyzing people to the best possible result is not always possible because some people are not entirely sincere about their body language. However, even seasoned psychologists can tell when somebody is telling a lie, and thus it is possible for anybody else if they make an effort. The simple fact remains that understanding how to analyze different people is an instrumental part of mastering social skills and forms the basis of better interactions. Body language cues are the most common ways of "reading" people as it allows you to use your intuition.

Chapter 7: Face Reading

Face reading is an intriguing method of analyzing other people because it focuses entirely on the expressions appearing on the face. In several instances by psychologists, they have attained success in determining character traits just from face reading, and some have been able to come up with diagnoses for behavioral problems. The concept of face reading is not new, however, and it forms an essential part in understanding the basic social skills. Learning to interpret the facial expressions of others is a crucial part of how you interact with them.

Face reading can be very complicated, and maybe this is a reason why it is not very common. Psychologists will insist that only 'professionals' can successfully conduct face reading exercises because they are trained to do so. They would probably be right because there are five main pitfalls associated with face reading that might be necessary to know when attempting to do so. Understanding these pitfalls will help improve your judgment of other people just from their facial expressions and enable you to master crucial social skills:

An expression may mean two different things: It is completely possible to misread a facial expression because it might mean two different things at once. A wink might be a gesture from a prospective lover who wants to have a conversation at that moment; the same facial expression can also be a gesture for you to leave with the person, and it is probably going to be accompanied by shaking of the head. Therefore, this confusion has made many people mistake a facial expression for a specific meaning, and it can often get awkward.

Complete misinterpretation: A person might opt to assume a facial expression is the total opposite of what it actually is, even though the facial expression has more than one meaning. One might take shaking of the head to mean that a person is happy when the opposite is true. Such mistakes are common and can be a hindrance to socializing because they create tense moments. It is necessary to be more patient and observe somebody before settling for their facial expressions because a misinterpretation will be the difference between a successful interaction and a failed one.

Extreme temperatures: Some people are too quick to judge character simply by looking once at the person and immediately making a conclusion. Funnily enough, extreme temperatures do affect the facial expression on somebody's face, and if you are quick to make a judgment, you will miss what they are actually feeling. When it is too hot or too cold, somebody can easily interpret the facial expression on your face to denote displeasure, and this can create an awkward scenario. Sometimes the opposite is true, and it is possible to assume that the person is happy; either way, it is necessary to observe this pitfall before concluding an analysis on a person on this basis.

Faking a facial expression to throw off another person: This is also a common practice among people who have something to hide. Some people will fake their facial expressions to avoid having discussions about either their disappointment or joy. Some people will behave like they are happy, but after speaking to them, you come to realize that they are actually sad and even sarcastic about it. Others are likely to have a sad expression on their faces, but in reality, they are very happy and just do not want to talk about it.

Unfamiliarity with certain facial expressions: Some people simply do not understand some facial expressions. This can be a serious disadvantage because it will be impossible to understand them – the chances of offending somebody because of failing to understand their facial expressions can be disastrous in an interaction. It usually helps when the facial expression made is understandable, but it is very possible to get lost during social interactions if you do not understand a facial expression. As a consequence, people are likely to talk about you right in front of you without you even knowing it.

The following is a list of facial expressions that are useful to know as they help in improving mastery of social skills:

Stroking the chin: This is an obvious facial expression that shows the person is deep in thought, and it might be best if they were not interrupted. When in a social setting, it will be advisable to be courteous to such a person. Approaching them slowly and politely will be the most appropriate way of interacting with them, and be mindful about keeping the chitchat to a minimum.

Pursed lips: This is a common facial expression for anybody experiencing bitter emotions and even anger. It would be best to approach such a person carefully because their emotions might implode at any moment. For instance, a person seated by themselves in a social gathering with pursed lips may best be left alone if you have no idea what to say to them. However, if you are in the mood to console them, you might find a way of interacting with them, and it will be up to you to improve their mood and make them smile.

Nodding: You are probably speaking to somebody who is in a good mood or in agreement with you if they are constantly nodding. This is a sign that the message being relayed is acceptable, and that they also approve of your company because they are openly expressing themselves. A nod is likely to be accompanied by a smile and other forms of body language that indicates agreement. It is easy to interact with such a person because they are openly receptive and likely to engage in conversation more easily.

Crow's feet: This is a big smile on the face that can sometimes almost stay permanent if a person is in a good mood. It is called crow's feet because it forms running lines across the face that look like the infamous bird's legs. A person with this facial expression is more likely to be open and in a good mood, and it should be simple enough for you to interact with them. A happy facial expression opens the door to conversation and happy interactions, and this is always a good character trait that introverts look for in prospective friends at social gatherings.

Smacking the lips: This is usually indicative of appreciation or general delight at what is currently happening. Smacking the lips shows obvious acknowledgment to something nice, and the person is usually in a good mood. If delicious food is laid on the table at an interactive party, several people are likely to smack their lips as they eagerly anticipate the delicious meal. The same applies when somebody sees a beautiful person – they might smack their lips in appreciation of the person's beauty, and this is a positive facial expression. When you observe somebody in this state, it becomes quite simple to interact with them.

Deep frown lines: This facial expression suggests that somebody is unhappy or deep in thought. The deep frown lines appear clearly on the face and influence a negative look. Interacting with such a person must be done quickly because they probably do not want to engage in conversation for a long time. It is necessary to be observant of this facial expression as it will help reduce the chances of approaching the person and offending them. If you see somebody sporting this facial expression, do not expect the happiest of conversations with them.

Clenched jaw/teeth: Somebody who clenches their teeth are probably nervous, angry and/or agitated. For the most part, this can be a sign of frustration, and clenching the teeth or jaw is just one way for the person to cope with the problem. They might not want to talk much judging from their facial expression, and so it might be necessary to keep interactions to a minimum.

Winking: Somebody who is winking at you might be trying to communicate that they like you and might be interested in talking to you. However, winking is a diverse facial expression, and it is possible to wink to denote direction or just simply grabbing your attention. When the opposite sex winks at you, it is fairly obvious what their intentions are; however, when a close friend of yours winks at you, they might be trying to get your attention or just simply motioning to you. Either way, it is an important facial expression which everybody understands and makes it easier for people to interact with one another.

Shaking of the head: This is a tell-tale sign that somebody is not happy or they do not approve of something. If you happen to be at a social gathering and see somebody shaking their head rigorously and continuously, they probably do not accept something they are being told. The shaking of the head is a surefire indication of disagreement, and it can easily prevent further interactions among people. It is also possible that somebody is mourning a loss, and this can be done by shaking the head. Interacting with this person must be done in a considerate manner because they are not in the best of moods.

Chapter 8: The Four Personality Types

The four personality traits that have commonly been used to distinguish among the temperaments of different people are choleric, sanguine, phlegmatic and melancholic. Hippocrates was among the earliest to describe these four personality types as personality traits and behaviors affected by four bodily fluids. The early Greeks had managed to coin these personality types as temperaments, and they used them to distinguish among people from their character and traits. In the modern world, the four personality types have been used to categorize people accordingly.

Galen was another important philosopher who was responsible for coming up with the personality types by linking them to physical conditions in the world. According to him, the four personality types could be linked to dry/wet and hot/cold situations. These earthly substances were linked to the temperament of a person and used as a basis for coming up with the personality types. Bodily humor played a significant role in determining the four personality types and quickly became associated with everybody. Medical science has progressed since and the personality traits are used by psychologists today to great effect to understand each person and provide an apt diagnosis.

Different aspects of personality are responsible for determining each of the four temperaments. However, it is not unusual for a person to display more than one type of personality trait depending on their mood and what type of activity they are engaged in. There is no standard combination for any of the personality traits as it is impossible to pinpoint to a person's temperaments. Linking each of the personality traits to an element in the world makes it easier to understand the inspiration behind it and the actual personality trait of the person:

Choleric

A choleric personality is one which describes a decisive and independent person who is driven to achieve specific objectives. Such people are usually extroverts and enjoy interacting with others as this is an important aspect of how they socialize. Such people tend to be leaders because they are constantly setting goals for themselves, and they also tend to be outgoing but not shy. This personality trait can be linked to brash leaders who are always at the forefront of attention and looking to provide guidance to everybody else.

One of the major characteristics of this personality type is that the person is usually outgoing and ambitious in their nature. Such people are always looking to discover and lead by example, and it is very difficult not to notice them in society because they make an effort to be seen. This personality type is linked to fire as a comparison to one of the elements in the world, and this signifies the ability of the person to rule over others. People who have this personality trait also like having a fact-based opinion of the world. They are also very straightforward in their views.

A good example of a choleric personality type is a leader such as Donald Trump who enjoys being at the head of any social and professional group he is involved in. He is very goal-oriented and will pursue his interests with intense vigor while at the same time emphasizing his leadership skills and the need for everybody to support him. Trump is a typical choleric leader because he also looks at the world from a fact-based approach and it is not easy to convince him otherwise. His personality trait also characterizes decisiveness as well as ambition as he has come to be known throughout the country.

Sanguine

A sanguine personality is described as one that is very active, social, and enthusiastic. A person with this personality type is easy to talk to because they enjoy it, and they are never satisfied with doing nothing. It is quite difficult to find such a person seated by themselves without anything to do because they are always all over the place. The noisemaker of the classroom tends to be sanguine because they are rarely calm and 'to themselves'. They enjoy interacting with others greatly, and they can be 'the life of the party' because their liveliness can be infectious.

The talkative nature of such people is an important characteristic that marks out a sanguine personality. They enjoy being part of a crowd, and they are very social people who are easy to approach and interact with. Sanguine personalities tend to be charismatic, and this can explain why several people like this specific personality type. Similarly, this personality type describes an extrovert who is more likely to be at a social gathering than at home alone. The earth element linked to this personality type is air, and it signifies the social usefulness of the person.

An example of a character that can be linked to this personality trait would be a celebrity like Justin Bieber. A person such as this would enjoy the company of others and even be a daredevil when in the company of friends. Such a person enjoys risky activity and will probably engage in a risky activity faster than they will have time to think about it. Such a person would enjoy performing at parties and generally hanging out with everybody and getting to know every single individual at the event.

Phlegmatic

This personality type differs significantly from the first two as it describes a person who is relaxed, peaceful and quiet. Such people are more composed and would prefer their own company rather than hanging out at a noisy place with lots of people. A phlegmatic individual tends to be easygoing, and it would probably be interesting to interact with such a person because it would be a very calm and relaxed interaction. Such people would prefer to stay away from trouble, and they are known for generalizing their thoughts and opinions on most matters.

Some of the major characteristics of individuals who possess phlegmatic personality traits are that they tend to hide their emotions and keep to themselves. It is difficult to know what is going on in the head of a phlegmatic individual because they do not speak much and would rather conceal their feelings. However, they are sympathetic individuals who display typical characteristics of introverts and are well known for making compromises. Such people tend to be very caring and openly receptive to other people. The element linked to this personality trait is water, and it describes a person who usually focuses on getting what they want in a reserved manner.

A good example of a person displaying this trait would be a primary school teacher. Most of these individuals tend to be sympathetic and understanding, particularly of young ones, and they spend a lot of time helping out their students to be better people. Classroom teachers sometimes do not speak much and only do so when the situation is absolutely necessary. The classroom teacher will be open to engaging with their students but only as much as they can assist them appropriately. They will not be overly outgoing, but they will be receptive enough, particularly to the students and open for interaction.

Melancholic

People who feel very deeply, and think in the same manner, display melancholic personalities. They are even quieter and reserved than phlegmatic people, and they tend to spend a lot of time by themselves lost in their own little worlds. They have very active brains, and they are known to be very creative because they spend a lot of time thinking. Individuals who possess this personality type are very analytical and take everything with the seriousness it deserves; they like details and would likely understand absolutely everything about the things that surround them.

Some of the major characteristics of this personality type include self-reliance and reservation that makes them unique from the rest of the population. It is not usually easy to spot a melancholic individual because they tend to avoid being singled out in a crowd, even if it means awkwardly mingling with those around them. As a classic introvert personality type, melancholic people tend to strive for perfection, and this usually results in them being very organized. The element that represents this trait is earth, and it signifies somebody who avoids too much interaction with the rest of the group.

A good example of individuals who display this character trait would be book authors such as Stephen King. They tend to be thinkers who spend a lot of time to themselves and are constantly organizing their thoughts to come up with different deals. Stephen King is a person very much reserved to himself and enjoys the time he spends alone as it offers him an opportunity to think of new book ideas. Stephen King is less likely to attend a party and more likely to be very tidy and detailed because his profession demands this of him.

Understanding the different personality types is instrumental in ensuring that you master the social skills necessary for interacting with everybody else. Comprehending the different personality types makes it even easier to analyze people from their body language and facial expressions. It becomes possible to make accurate judgments about somebody's character and preferences, thereby minimizing the chances of making mistakes when interacting with the individual. A key part of developing your social skills is learning to differentiate between the different personality types as it allows you to understand the manner of interaction to engage with each person.

Chapter 9: How to Detect a Liar

In the process of social interaction, it is possible to come across liars who will try to derail your understanding. Such people are not uncommon in a social gathering, and there are also liars in a professional setting. The important thing for you is to understand when a liar is in action so that you are not misguided as it can cause some embarrassment when interacting with other people. The truth is always important, particularly when a decision must be made, and so understanding how to spot liars is extremely important.

Most people in society who have already mastered social skills are good at spotting liars from tell-tale signs. Liars behave in a specific way, and it is possible to tell from their body language and facial expressions. Factors such as the tone of their voice and interactions with other people are also indicative of a liar, and it is advantageous to spot one to avoid being misled. Psychologists have developed several methods of spotting liars in a social situation, and the following methods are useful in ensuring you keep away from such individuals:

Staring but not blinking: if you want to attain a mastery of social skills, it is important to distinguish between a truthful person and a liar. Most liars usually do not blink when staring at you because they want to be as convincing as possible. They will give you a cold, hard stare in an attempt to make you believe that what they are saying is honest. In reality, however, the cold, hard look has been forced on in order for you to believe that they are quite serious with what they are saying. They will likely maintain this stance for as long as possible provided you appear to be following their story.

Hands stay out of sight: This is a common trait among liars where they tend to keep their hands directly away from your sight as they try to tell you something. Psychologists attribute this behavior to the basis that one is trying to hide something, and they are likely to indicate it through some form of body language. The fact is, a liar will be hiding something away from you as they tell you one thing when, in fact, it is the opposite. Detecting this type of liar will require you to have some understanding of the basic body language expressions.

Repetition: This is another interesting trait of a liar because sometimes they might do it consciously or unconsciously. A liar will constantly repeat the lie because it is likely to sound true if it is said over and over again. They rely on familiarizing you with the lie as frequently as possible so that it becomes 'normal' to you. They can also repeatedly lie unconsciously when telling a long, complicated lie and this usually exposes them in a social situation. Constant repetition will indicate the person is nervous and doing a difficult job trying to twist a narrative so that it sounds as real as possible.

Pausing for a long time: If you find that having a conversation with somebody is difficult because they are constantly pausing, it is highly likely that they are spending much of the time lying to you. Liars usually pause for long periods in order to prepare what they are going to say. Every statement they make in such an instance is tailor-made for the occasion, and they do so to conceal the truth and convince you of something different. Long pauses are quite concerning, and they leave the listener in doubt because it is almost impossible to have a single conversation continuously. The occasional interruptions because the person must think or pretends to have zoned out is indicative of a deceptive character. It is necessary to be observant around such a person because it is highly likely that most of the things they are going to say will be far from the truth. A truthful person will be able to keep up with a conversation without frequent pauses because there is not much to think about but speak with an open mind.

Talking too much: Somebody who is also speaking too rapidly to give you time to contribute to the conversation is probably lying. Giving away too much information when having a simple discussion can be indicative of a lying personality. It is necessary to be careful with such a person because they will focus on bombarding you with too much information for you to think of anything else. This is dangerous because they can transform simple statements into believable words when they are, in fact, the opposite of what they actually mean. Be wary of somebody who speaks too much because the value of what they are saying might not be worthwhile.

Rubbing the chin and mouth: A nervous person who is trying to get away with something is usually twitchy and very much on edge. Having a conversation with somebody who is constantly rubbing their chin and covering their mouth might show that they are hiding something. Consequently, the conversation you will have with them might not be a frank one because of the person's need to hide the actual facts. Covering the mouth usually symbolizes the need to be quiet and keep the actual facts away from a statement.

Strange body language: It is likely that somebody is telling you they are fine and well when they are nervously twitching and jerking. Body language is an important expression that can help anybody looking to master social skills spot a liar. A person can say one thing, but it is very possible that their body will communicate something entirely different, signifying that they are lying. When somebody speaks to you, pay attention to the way they are positioned and any strange movements they make. This might be the difference between you knowing whether they are being honest with you or not.

High-pitched voice/laughter: A person speaking with a very high-pitched voice and laughing very loudly is probably nervous because they are trying to hide something. This is particularly suspicious if there is no call for being loud in any way. The high-pitched voice is probably trying to drown out the conflict in the liar's head because they know that whatever they are saying is not truthful. The high-pitched laughter also covers for the fact that they are faking their laughter in an attempt to fit in and lure you away from the truth.

Sudden movements with the head: A person who is lying will make sudden movements with the head, particularly when they are making a false statement or opposing something with you. They might jerk their heads because they are trying to hide the fact that they are being dishonest with what they are saying. These sudden movements are suspicious, particularly when having a normal conversation, and they should show you that somebody is trying to hide some truth. If you make an accusation against them, they are also likely to jerk their heads because they are trying to fight with the truth and they know it.

Clearing the throat a lot: If it is almost impossible to have a conversation with somebody because they are constantly clearing their throat, it is indicative of them hiding something. Clearing the throat is a signature way of secretly communicating to somebody else that you are telling a blatant lie. Be wary of somebody who is constantly clearing their throat in conversation even if they are healthy because it is likely that what they are talking about is not truthful. In such an instance, you are better walking away from such a conversation than bearing the continuous throat-clearing exercise.

Shuffling of the feet: Somebody who is telling a lie and is nervous about it will constantly be shuffling the feet in a bid to make themselves as comfortable as possible. They will be scared as what they are saying is dishonest, and they will move about and be fidgety. Their nervousness will be obvious to see because they will not be comfortable being around you or engaging in conversation. Instead, they are probably going to be more of a flight risk because they will not want to hang around long after telling their lies.

Avoiding/ignoring some questions: Liars will often avoid questions or statements of fact by changing the subject or simply remaining quiet. If you find that you are speaking to somebody but they are constantly changing the topic and you find yourselves speaking about something else, they are probably concealing a lie. This is an important aspect of understanding social skills because it is necessary to spot those who behave very nervously under pressure. When somebody ignores your question, you might as well end your interaction because you cannot be sure anything else they say will be honest.

Aggression: Some liars get overly aggressive particularly when they are called on what they are saying. Instant aggression is a good sign that you are talking to a liar because it shows that they are willing to go to great extents to cover up information. Aggressive behaviors compensate for the lack of ideas because the individual has no choice but to forcefully back whatever they are saying even though it has already been debunked. A truthful person will always maintain their cool even when they are being discredited because they have nothing to hide.

Failing to deny: If somebody goes as far as refusing to be honest, even though new information has been revealed to show that they were not accurate, then this is indicative of a liar. Total rejection of somebody else's opinion and sticking to a path that everybody else is opposing shows that the person you are dealing with is not honest. A truthful person never conceals information when asked because they have no reason to twist the reality; whereas a liar will have something to hide. Therefore, they will fail to deny, in some instances, repetitively, and this will show their true nature.

The most important thing associated with understanding the nature of a liar is that it enables you to boost your mastery of social skills, and it becomes difficult for other people to tell you otherwise. The objective of detecting a liar is to prevent being lied to, but it also offers an excellent opportunity for you to understand people better. This chapter links with Chapter 5, which provided information on analyzing people, because true mastery of social skills depends on the understanding of these basic facts. Use the information provided in this chapter to your advantage to determine whether it is worthwhile to interact with some individuals based on their ability to be honest.

Chapter 10: Make Body Language your Superpower

Getting your body language right can be very useful in the process of mastering good social skills. This is because it is possible to communicate very effectively with other people by way of body language, particularly when what you say aligns with the motions of your body. A good mastery of body language can make you an instant hit because people will always associate their interactions with you by associating specific types of body language. For example, it is a fun way to interact with an umpire or referee in the real world by pointing at them for fun the same way they do when officiating a game.

Therefore, the following are practical tips on how body language can be used to advance your social skills:

Positivity is infectious: Many people might not be aware that by simply remaining positive, it has a corresponding effect on the people around them. Remaining positive can involve distinctive forms of body language such as moving about lightly, singing gently or interacting in a very friendly manner with everybody around you. Either way, it is an excellent way of improving social skills as it endears you to everybody around you.

A good example of this is taking a morning run where you say hello to everybody and wave at them happily. This sense of joy is likely to infect everybody, from the postman to the ordinary people going about their duties. Taking a run through town in this kind of attitude is an excellent way to show the importance of having positive body language constantly. This is because it makes everybody else feel the need to emulate you, particularly when responding to you.

Dressing colorfully and flashily: How people dress and present themselves is crucial to determining their social interactions. It is quite rare to find somebody interacting with the garbage collector hard at work because the conditions around them might be deplorable. In the same respect, it is very possible to interact easily with a flashily dressed attendant at a restaurant because they have caught your eye and left you with several questions. Dressing well and matching it with positive body movements, such as gracefully walking, ends up being an important determiner in your mastery of social skills.

A good example of this can be seen when somebody is going to work and is dressed appropriately and exuding positivity. A pilot, for instance, walking through a crowd in the airport not only draws respect because of his or her profession but also their attire as well. With a smile on their face and a spring in their step, he or she is likely to spread that positivity easily, and everybody in the vicinity would not mind interacting with them. Outward presentation is an essential part of body language that can make you likable among several people, thereby helping you tremendously to boost your social skills.

Constantly smiling and offering a firm handshake: Another way that body language can improve social skills immediately is by smiling and happily shaking hands with other people. Smiling is an integral element of body language and a basic facial expression that can guide people towards liking you. Extroverts who are constantly socializing understand the secret to smiling, and they do it to keep the attention of several people at once. A firm handshake is equally important because several people take pride in this and use it immediately to judge somebody.

A good example of this is a customer representative who has to meet with several clients in a day. The business the representative is conducting will be successful if they can handle as many clients as possible, satisfying them successfully and ensuring that backlog is kept to a minimum. A customer representative can achieve this simple, standard goal by smiling with their customers whenever they walk up to them and offering a firm handshake. A weak handshake sometimes denotes disinterest from the person, and so it is important that the customer service representative makes the client feel as welcome as possible.

Hand gestures: This type of body language is particularly useful when trying to explain something technical to a single person or group of people. Hand gestures help to show emphasis at different points of conversation, and this highlights what is important and noteworthy. It is simple for another person to follow what you are telling them because you are providing descriptive guides by using your hands and motioning in different ways. Hand gestures are a basic form of body language and a crucial way of discussing technical matters that require demonstration to make them easier to comprehend.

A good example of this is when you are introducing a new product before your company's board members and trying to get them to sell it. You are likely to make a PowerPoint presentation where you highlight different merits of the products, its price, and the associated business expenses. When having this technical conversation, you will use hand gestures at different points of the presentation, for instance pointing at the profits to emphasize the likely benefit that the company will enjoy in the near future. Hand gestures are instrumental in helping to show what is important by matching them with speech, and this helps in improving social skills immensely.

Rubbing the hands together: This is another type of body language that can help you improve your social skills. When communicating with somebody, you can rub your hands to indicate anticipation of something good, particularly when you match it with speech. Rubbing your hands together will ensure the listener remains calm and on your side because they can also feel the positivity you are exuding. It shows that you have confidence in what you are pursuing and that you can give a fairly accurate forecast of what is about to happen.

A good example of this is when delivering news to an expectant father. If he is waiting outside a maternity room and the doctor appears, he can rub his hands as he approaches the father with a smile on his face. The father might not even have to ask because, from the body language of the physician, it is likely that he has good news for him. Rubbing the hands in such a manner shows that there is positive anticipation to account for and that the father should have every reason to be a happy man.

Leaning in one direction: This is another telling type of body language because it involves positioning your body towards something you like, with the opposite being true. If you like somebody and you are on a romantic date, you might find yourself leaning closer towards them. An interesting person will have something nice to say, and they will constantly keep your attention, hence explaining the positioning of your body. If somebody is uncomfortable or not speaking the truth, they might lean away from you as a form of protection and also in the hope that you will not realize what they are concealing.

A good example of this is a romantic date where the positioning of your body can tell whether the evening is going well or not. If you find that the opposite sex is spending a lot of time trying to get closer to you, this could mean that they really like you and would like to hang onto everything you say. Their body positioning can easily tell you everything you need to know about your social skills because they will show their displeasure or pleasure with their body movements.

Speaking while exposing your palms: This is another important form of body language that expresses innocence to emphasize that what you are speaking is the truth. This is a gesture that is used on several occasions, and it always shows that the speaker is willing to be called on what they are saying. It is a sign of sincerity, but liars can also use this body language gesture to justify anything they are saying. Typically, this gesture can even be used to indicate surrender, whether it is an actual conflict or simply in conversation. Understanding this basic hand gesture is important towards boosting your social skills.

A good example of when this gesture is put into practice is when somebody is trying to justify a basic truth. For instance, if you are trying to tell a friend that Alaska is part of the United States, you are likely to expose your palms with a slight shrug of the shoulders to indicate that you are telling the truth. Similarly, worshipers usually raise their hands and expose their palms to the sky symbolic of the fact that they surrender to God's will and will worship His name. This hand gesture shows innocence and a willingness to accept what is before us.

Nodding and shaking the head: An excellent way of keeping a conversation going without interrupting it is by nodding and shaking the head. These are important body language expressions that are very standard and basic to understand. Nodding is indicative of agreement where a conversation can keep going as long as the listeners are nodding. This silently acknowledges the fact that they are listening while at the same time agreeing with the points being presented. When the listeners shake their heads, it can be either that the speaker was not audible enough or they oppose a point that has been raised.

A good example of this can be seen when a group of people is strategizing and trying to put different parts of a plan together. When the speaker explains the basic parts of the plan, everybody will nod and keep up with the conversation. However, when something is said, and the majority of the people do not agree, they will shake their heads, and disgruntlement is likely to follow. These simple body movements can help improve social skills because they ensure efficiency even in the simplest of conversation.

Chapter 11: Handling Small Talk as an Introvert

An introvert is a person who prefers to keep their own company in a peaceful surrounding. This is a stark contrast to an extrovert who prefers the tumultuous company of several friends in a lively environment. This shows that introverts are poor at handling small talk because they rarely engage in it and only do so in the company of very close friends. Most introverts are deep, meaningful people and are always looking to be talking about something interesting. Some of the topics that introverts talk about range from changing the world, bringing peace everywhere, and conspiracy theories. Introverts are always unique minded people that have no interest in the system and the current order of things. They always think big, and as a result, some of the actions they take can attract more attention than they believed so. Introverts do not find the process of socializing and even engaging in small talk as fun – in any way. An introvert would rather discuss an upcoming business plan than spend an hour engaging in small talk that will bring no significant benefit at the end of the day.

Why is small talk difficult and desirable for introverts?

It is a waste of time: Introverts do not take much pride in wasting time talking over matters that have already been said. Instead of seeing the appeal of simply discussing something casually with friends, an introvert would rather spend that time more constructively to gain something at the end of the day. For example, an introvert would rather discuss a plot for the next book they want to publish as opposed to chitchatting about the latest celebrity on the news.

Socializing is tiring: Introverts find it difficult to sit around and have long conversations that are not particularly beneficial because it is tiring. As mentioned, they prefer to have deeper, meaningful conversations and keep the small talk to a minimum. They also find it difficult trying to fit into crowds they already know are a poor fit.

Introverts have a smaller circle of friends that they are comfortable with for small talk: Introverts usually have a tightly-knight friendship with a few people, and it is probable to find them engaging in small talk with their friends. However, when it comes to engaging with other people, it is difficult because there is a lack of understanding between the two sets of people. Introverts want to talk about specific things and will be interested in new ideas and information. Small talk, though, is not desirable because it is not as interesting as it is speaking with their friends, making it undesirable for them.

There is little desire among introverts to master social skills: Introverts are barely interested in keeping up with the basic social skills that would otherwise make it easier to engage in small talk. Introverts would rather interact with close friends and enjoy a stimulating environment because they find it tiring and a waste of time engaging in small talk. Their little desire to improve their social skills contributes to the difficulty they experience just sitting down for a few minutes and having a light conversation. A mastery of social skills can make all the difference in tolerating and even enjoying small talk.

Preference for their own little worlds: Small talk is a daunting task for introverts because they are constantly locked in their own little worlds and would prefer to stay there. Small talk has no place for their little worlds because the latter usually is the most comfortable place for an introvert. An extrovert, however, would not mind engaging in small talk to relax because they can manifest their personality. Therefore, the fact that introverts are usually lost within themselves makes it difficult for them even to concentrate when others are engaging in small talk.

The following are practical tips on how an introvert can tackle the problems associated with small talk:

Nodding to keep attention: There is nothing wrong with nodding along when somebody else is speaking because it means that you are attentive and agree with them. The essence of small talk is to engage in a manner that does not create conflict, and thus nodding along, regardless of what is being said, is one way an introvert can keep up. It is better to nod along than be rude and openly show your disinterest in the subject because patience is an essential element of mastering social skills.

Trying to change the subject subtly: It is also all right to try and introduce a new subject of conversation in order for you to genuinely participate in the conversation. As an introvert, you will be driven to discuss something that is of meaning, and there is nothing wrong with getting the rest of the people involved. However, it is important to change the subject slowly and respectfully because you do not want to imply that what everybody is engaging in is a waste of time. Instead, be subtle about introducing a new topic that will make you feel participative.

Asking questions to try to keep up interest: Another good tactic is asking questions at different points during the small talk to spike your interest. This is likely to show your host that you are not knowledgeable on the subject, and they will end up sharing intricate details and spike your interest. Asking questions will also reveal little things that you did not know, and this will end up drawing you in to socialize with the rest of the people. Appreciating the essence of small talk can begin by asking friendly questions that help to enlighten you.

Soliciting a friend's help to keep up: It is possible to ask a friend to give you information when engaged among a group in small talk. A close friend can help you keep up and even appreciate the conversation by pointing out different things and answering your questions. Having a friend along makes the situation a bit easier because you can have some practical guidance on how to interact with the rest of the people. With time, small talk stops becoming difficult and undesirable because you have gotten used to it and have been guided appropriately.

Venture into common small talk topics: It might be that you are familiar with common small talk topics that you can engage in, maybe political gossip or sports. Sometimes it helps when you steer the conversation in this direction as it will provide you with a topic that you can mutually discuss with other people. This is an effective way of getting around the boredom created by small talk because you can try and talk about something you are more familiar with. This way, the monotony associated with small talk will reduce, and it will be possible to see it as a positive way of interacting.

Crack a joke: Another equally effective way of getting around the problem of the boredom created by small talk is cracking a joke. This is a common way of breaking the ice in several social interaction instances, and it will do the trick if you're trying to fit in among a group engaged in small talk. It will draw the approval of everybody else, particularly if you tell a good joke, and it will enable you to be a part of the group on the basis of your contribution.

Tell an interesting fact: It is possible to completely change the dynamics of small talk by talking about something real and interesting. This will draw the attention of everybody and become the new subject of conversation. Telling an interesting fact is just as important as changing the subject because it gives you control over the conversation and you can decide what everybody else will talk about. Give an interesting fact such as the largest aircraft in the world; such topics will solicit the interest of everybody else and will give you the chance to engage in much more interesting small talk, thereby getting around the problem.

Speak about an interesting travel experience: This is another way of getting around the problems presented by engaging in small talk. Instead of having to talk about a topic that you find boring and unhelpful, it might be better to talk about different parts of the world. This is an excellent social approach to improving your social skills because you can connect with different people who have shared interests. It is very rare to be in a group of people who have no interest in travel because people are constantly talking about other parts of the world. It is possible to avoid the difficulty and undesirability associated with small talk by introducing interesting travel topics about exotic places in the world.

Do not remain silent, no matter what: Somebody who does not contribute to the conversation will quickly be seen as boring because they are doing nothing. This is the wrong way of approaching the issues associated with small talk because as much as it can be tedious, it is better to say something than remain quiet. Silence can be a direct implication that everybody around you is boring, and this will be the wrong way of approaching the challenges of small talk.

Kindly excuse yourself: It is not rude to kindly excuse yourself and walk away when people start small talk. However, what is important is to excuse yourself decently, so you don't spark anybody's attention or seem offensive. There are many ways in which one can excuse themselves, but it is always best to apologize as you stand up to leave. A respectful exit from the place will earn you a future place among the friends whenever you are ready to hang out with them.

Chapter 12: Introvert Problems and Relationships

Introverts face many challenges as a result of lacking social skills that enable them to make more friends. This is also true in the dating field where they struggle to woo mates as compared to their extrovert friends who can woo as many mates as possible. The opposite sex has always been a subject of conversation for introverts because they are constantly seeking the best way of approaching them and confessing their love. However, whenever they do get an opportunity to do this, it comes off badly, and they end up embarrassing themselves.

When setting up a date, it is important to consider the following factors:

Choose a scenic location that both of you approve: It is important to go out on a first date to a scenic location that has meaning for both of you. This can be a restaurant or a national park; either way, it is important that the place has meaning because it will help establish a connection between the two of you. A good first date is essential in determining whether a relationship will be successful, and so extra attention must be paid into that first impression.

Talk about shared interests: The most efficient way that you can keep up with a conversation while out on a date is by talking about shared interests. Get to know your date a little more, and you will find that he or she is open to discussing subjects that are of interest to you. If they are a historian, talking about the history of the country and tackling old-age dilemmas might be an excellent way for you to connect. You will find yourself speaking freely, and you will derive happiness as a result of spending your time constructively.

Do not bring up sex so soon: This is a common mistake among guys who are too quick to bring up sex and quickly discourages the opposite sex. When it comes to a meaningful date, it is important to take your mate slowly and allow him or her to get to know you more. You will be surprised that after only a short wait, he or she will suggest it. Do not make the mistake of rashly bringing up sex or setting any conditions because that is likely to ruin the relationship that has already been established.

Avoid long pauses: Remember that when it is a date, it is just the two of you. Do not bore your mate by remaining quiet and handling the conversation because it is important that you equally contribute. A date will be more successful if you both contribute to the conversation and try to interest each other. Do not be too focused on trying to make the date as memorable as possible because this is likely to distract you from your mate. If you are going to pause, stare deeply into their eyes and let them know that your full attention is on them.

Use respectful language: Before you know somebody well, it is always important to use respectful language and minimize the slang while on a date. Formality is important, and this will endear the opposite sex to you more than if you insist on using disrespectful language. How you present yourself to a date is important in determining whether you have a future because no one wants to hang around someone who is not properly cultured. Compose yourself throughout the evening and make sure that when you speak, you sound right.

Always be on time: This is another common mistake that sometimes people make whenever they have a date. It is okay to run late once, maybe twice, but never make it a habit. It is extremely irritating and does nothing for your mastery of social skills because the opposite sex is likely to become fed up with waiting for you. Always keep time dates and do not make rash promises that will result in your date having to wait for you for extended periods. Value their time because wasting it while on a date is also ill-advised; pay full attention to them while you are together because if there is something to do, it can always be done some other time.

To have a successful conversation with the opposite sex, there are a number of factors to consider in order to instigate a personal conversation successfully:

Be gentle and respectful: It is of the utmost importance that you treat your date with careful regard and always consider their wishes highly as it will determine the bonds of your friendship. Most people think that acting brashly and noisily will impress your date, but nothing could be further from the truth. The opposite sex usually likes somebody who is calm because it makes it easier to approach them and talk privately. Be gentle and mindful of the people around you so that you don't offend your date because a private conversation should remain as such. Humble yourself and be close to your date so that you can talk softly and gently. This will be an excellent way of improving your social skills and securing a good friend.

Have constant communication: It is important to speak continuously to the opposite sex whenever you are not together, but be careful and do it respectfully. Know their routines so that you can have specific chat times during the day and in the evenings. Send each other messages to find out how the other is doing, and limit the conversations to casual talk and not technical talk. Being in constant communication means that you are thinking about one another and it will enable you to master the basic aspects of social skills.

Listen to their problems: You must always have an ear to listen to the problems being experienced by the opposite sex. It is a good way of opening up a personal conversation, but it is important that you are meaningful and understanding of the problems that they are experiencing. This is important because it shows that you truly care for them and enables you to master important social skills. Your empathy in such a situation will allow you to establish a much closer relationship with the person, and they will, in turn, be open to talking to you.

One-on-one conversations are just as important as over the phone: You should place a lot of value on communicating with your partner because it builds upon your trust for each other. One-on-one conversations are just as important as when you speak on the phone, so you have to keep it respectful. This also applies to messages, and it is necessary not to bombard the opposite sex with too much technical talk. Focus on speaking about them, their day, how they are feeling, and what you can do to make them feel better.

Minimize friends when having personal conversations: Sometimes you might always want your close friend beside you, even when you are on a date. While this is okay probably for one occasion, it should be something that is never attempted. You should take pride in the alone time that you spend with the opposite sex, and they will appreciate you more when you have enough time for them. Constantly having your friend when you are spending time with the opposite sex is an indication that you do not enjoy their time so much. This could easily spell the end of the relationship because you must always set aside time for being with the opposite sex away from your close friends.

Reciprocating in a romantic relationship is just as important as being respectful. There are a number of ways that you can achieve this:

Giving gifts: You should focus some of your time shopping to find some of the finest gifts that you can share with the opposite sex. Gift giving is a respectful action as it shows you value the other individual, and it is an excellent way of reciprocating their love to you. When you give gifts, you have to be mindful of their value and significance, so you don't offend the opposite sex.

Do not forget anniversaries and birthdays: Reciprocating somebody's love also involves being mindful of significant days in their lives and celebrating it with them. Anniversaries are important because they show the scope of a relationship, and it enables mutual respect to be established between the two of you. Birthdays are also an excellent way of showing love towards each other and making it a special occasion certainly boosts the love between the two. Basic practices such as these improve your social skills and enable you to be a sensitive and reasonable person to your mate.

Be there for them during hard times: Times of sorrow are typically the most challenging for any person, and thus having a friend who can be by your side is extremely important. If you show your mate support at a time when they are saddest, say someone has died in their family, it establishes strong bonds of friendship that are very difficult to break. It is a great social skill to be considerate and have empathy.

Do not cheat: It is also important not to make the mistake of being dishonest because this can destroy years of friendship. Unfaithfulness is one of the worst things that can happen to a relationship, and it can destroy years of hard work mastering social skills. Always be honest with your mate whenever you have a conversation and confide in them. This will allow you to build your trust and respect for one another with time, and pretty soon, you will never be uncomfortable around them. Developing good social skills is dependent on honesty, and the lack of it only guarantees the destruction of a relationship.

Respect family and friends: It is imperative to have absolute respect for the family and friends of your mate. This is paramount to achieving success in the relationship because it will make them like you even better. A relationship will become prosperous if each of you can approve the friends around your mate as this will be a sign of you joining that circle as well. Respect for the family will also make you be a part of it, and your mate will respect you even more as a result.

Chapter 13: Introvert Problems in an Open Workplace

Introverts behave uniquely in an open workplace because they are forced to interact with others while at the same time remaining reserved. One of the most important characteristics of an introvert is their pride in their alone time and an opportunity to disappear into their thoughts. An open workplace is perhaps one of the worst places an introvert would want to be because everybody has access to them. There is no time to think independently because they always have to work. Should they get a little free time to think for themselves, they are likely to be interrupted by the numerous people working in the office. It becomes a necessity for them to understand a few basic social skills in order to work with their colleagues and be a part of the larger business team. The process of learning social skills has always been a problem for introverts because they see it as a waste of time. Their behavior has always been unique as much as they have been accused of being vastly different from the rest of the population. However, it is important to discuss the specific way in which introverts behave in the open workplace as it will shed light on the social skills that need to be mastered.

Introverts keep to themselves: Even in an open workplace, introverts will try to reserve the tiny bit of independence they can. They have a well laid out workspace of which is like their own little world where they get their work done. They keep interactions to a minimum because they spend much of their time focused on their work, and they rarely engage in other activities. It is difficult to interact with them unless you approach them. Otherwise, they remain incredibly focused on their work.

They rarely engage in small talk: As previously mentioned, it is hard to find an introvert busy contributing to small talk, and this also applies in an open workplace. In fact, despite small talk being a standard way of interacting with other work colleagues, introverts prefer to keep to themselves and only speak when they have to. This is not to say they never engage in small talk, but it is a rarity compared to the rest of their extrovert work colleagues, and it easily singles them out in the workplace. Introverts are not chatty people, and the chances are high that they will be the quietest people in an office block.

They work best outside teams: Introverts prefer to do things by themselves, and this means that they never work well in teams. They would rather accomplish a project by controlling the main aspects of it and only solicit outside help for technical responsibilities. Introverts like taking full charge of a project and they rarely adopt a hands-on approach unless it is absolutely necessary. When working in teams, they might not contribute much in terms of speech, but they always get their share of the work done efficiently. Introverts are the lone wolves of the office who sometimes can be relied on as a last resort when handling difficult tasks.

They are tidy and precise: Introverts are surprisingly straightforward when interacting with their employees, and they are well organized as well. Since they keep personal discussions at a minimum, interactions with other employees are on the basis of their responsibilities. They can easily be singled out in the office for their tidiness and organization as compared to their extrovert colleagues who would rather spend free time with friends than organizing their desk compartments. Introverts also appreciate timeliness and are always the first to work every morning, maintaining that precision frequently.

They mainly engage in technical talk: When introverts do decide to engage in conversation, it will be business jargon and technical talk more than small talk. Introverts will always try to find usefulness in the way they spend their time, and this means passing it by talking about constructive subjects. They will probably try and solicit the assistance of their fellow employees in a project they are doing in the workplace, and they can also talk about different types of business opportunities. The conversations that are conducted by the introverts of the office tend to be different from the typical small talk that most are used to.

Quiet and reserved: This is the classic trait of the introvert in the workplace because they do not interact much with the people around them. Instead, they prefer to spend their time working on their projects and less time interacting with others. They are rarely involved in the affairs of other people and prefer to keep to themselves as much as possible. They can barely be heard even in group meetings because they rarely see the need to address a large crowd of people. If they do have a problem in the office, they will seek to resolve the issue with their supervisor or manager.

Excited by company projects: The introvert is always looking to further projects within the company and attain as much success as possible. This is a crucial passion for them and expresses a reason for their involvement in the workplace. An introvert takes their work very seriously and also takes pride in when their ideas prosper along with the company. This is another possible conversation item for introverts within the workplace because they will always be talking about new projects and promoting ideas that might change the dynamic of their surroundings.

Rarely attends parties and retreats: The classic introvert does not frequent office gatherings unless it is necessary. It is possible to fail to spot them at a party or a retreat because they would rather be spending their time more constructively. This would be the kind of opportunity that at extrovert embraces with all their might, but an introvert would rather be in a much calmer environment that they have control of. This behavior might seem anti-social, but it is just a classic characteristic of the introvert; understanding the important aspects of social skills will be crucial for change.

It is possible for the introvert to take action to excel in their social skills while at work. The following are practical tips that can help you while in the workplace:

Work in teams: One possible way that you can excel at social skills in your place of work is by being comfortable working in a team. This will give you the opportunity to interact with several people and have a chance to create bonds. Working in a team is special because you will get a chance to appreciate the contributions of each person and learn a thing or two about social interactions.

Forge stronger bonds with workmates: It is possible for you to forge stronger bonds with fellow workmates by identifying hobbies that you can both engage in. This can be anything, from playing chess to sharing funny stories. It is necessary to have a work colleague as a close friend but not necessarily in your closer circle of friends. Having a good friend at work can make all the difference in trying to master social skills that will make it much easier for you to interact with the rest of the office.

Spend time at retreats and parties: Another good way of ensuring that you spend as much time as possible with work colleagues is attending parties and work retreats. If you hear somebody is having a birthday party in the office, attend it and try to practice some of the small talk as mentioned earlier. It is an excellent way of broadening your social skills, and attending the corporate retreats, too, will be an excellent idea and a chance for improvement.

Active participation in staff meetings: It is important for your voice to be heard in the office, and one effective way of doing this is participating actively in staff meetings. This will give an opportunity not only to your work colleagues to notice you but management as well. Practicing formal ways of addressing others in the workplace should be looked up to provide a better picture of the expectations. Participation in the staff meetings will get you noticed and give an opportunity for others to approach you. This will be a good way of breaking the ice and furthering your social skills in a professional setting.

Read up some more about socializing in a work environment: The internet is awash with several articles that will provide information about active ways of participating in the office. This will broaden your understanding and enable you to find definitions to terms you were not aware of. Reading up on the subject will give you theoretical knowledge from which you can practice by being more active in the workplace. Diversify your sources of information as this will prove important in finding the right advice about social skills. Reading will enable you to identify the challenges you experience and offer you an opportunity to research the solution.

Organizing get-togethers: It is also all right to take the initiative and organize an event that brings work colleagues together. This would prove to be a success because work colleagues will never forget a display of kindness and will constantly talk about it in the office. This will be an excellent way for you to boost your reputation and interact with people you normally would not. It will also help in establishing a good reputation in the office, and such an experience can easily increase your mastery of social skills in a professional setting.

Having a positive outlook: It is important to exude positivity while in the office because it will rub off on others to ensure a good working atmosphere. Talking with a smile on your face and being courteous to everybody else are important traits in ensuring that relations are excellent. In the work environment, you can greatly improve your social skills simply by being polite and helpful. Other work colleagues appreciate kindness and positivity and will often reciprocate goodwill to the benefit of everybody working there.

Chapter 14: Introvert Problems at Social Gatherings, Events, and Parties

Social gatherings, events, and parties can be one of the worst destinations for introverts. This is because they are forced to interact with other people and be in an environment where they feel out of place. Yet these events are important for work colleagues to pass on important information and to give them a chance to interact on a friendly basis. There are a number of measures an introvert can take to improve their social skills to fit in among crowds. However, it is important first to understand the challenges that introverts face in such situations:

Stage fright: This is a serious problem that faces any introvert because they are not used to taking to the stage and addressing a large number of people. Stage fright is a serious problem that hampers the delivery of any message that an introvert has because most people will be paying attention to their follies. This problem sometimes overcomes the speech ability of the individual, and they end up standing on stage for minutes on end either saying nothing or just stammering incomprehensible words. This happens as a result of having to face too many people at once, something that most introverts are not used to.

Discomfort engaging in small talk: The main type of conversation at a party or event will be characterized by small talk. Thus, introverts will be very uncomfortable in such a setting because they are not familiar with small talk and neither do they have an interest in it. They are uncomfortable needlessly contributing to a conversation they are not interested in, and they are likely to spend their time wandering about looking for something interesting.

Too many unfamiliar faces: Introverts are very uncomfortable around people they do not know, and the fact that their social skills are not the best does not help the situation. Too many unfamiliar faces usually make most introverts coil up in silence because they have nothing to speak about to a stranger. This is a contrast to an extrovert who will relish the opportunity to meet somebody new and talk to them. The fact that there are too many faces that the introvert is not familiar with makes it a problem for them to be at the party.

Opposite of a relaxed environment: Parties, events and social gatherings are the opposite of what an introvert might consider comfortable. This is because they prefer relaxed, serene environments where they can have a chance to disappear into their thoughts and own little world. This is not possible at a party because of all the distractions, and this makes it a serious problem for such character types.

Too much noise: Events are always noisy occasions, and introverts do not like such environments. If you are an introvert, you will try to complete your business at such gatherings as fast as possible so that you can return to the peace of your home. Noisy places make it is almost impossible to think clearly or make rational decisions in all the mayhem. It is far much more preferable being in a silent place with minimal interruption than to be in a flashy party with all the noise and activity around you.

Drifting off/boredom: It is easy for an introvert to get bored at an event, particularly if they do not know too many people or have an interest in what is being spoken about. Since they will be keeping interactions to a minimum, it is highly possible that they will want to leave as soon as possible because they'll be wasting their time. Such events can be time-consuming, and if they feel that they are not getting any value from them, they are likely to drift off easily. This is another serious problem that introverts have to deal with constantly as a result of having to attend social gatherings.

Spending too much time practicing: There is nothing wrong with planning, but spending too much time doing it can be catastrophic. As much as mastering social skills is important, it is necessary that it is done in moderation to avoid any nervousness. The process of learning social skills should be fun because it will be based on an introvert's experiences. Having a friend to help is always a good idea because they will act as a useful guide as the introvert sharpens their skills of interaction. They should take note of the time they spend in front of a mirror to prevent making themselves nervous and spoiling hours of good work.

Exhausting: Socializing can be very tiring for an introvert, particularly if they are not used to it. Events involve walking around, greeting several strangers and forcing conversations with them. They might also have to talk in front of a large group of people, and maintaining their interest in the event might prove to be a significant challenge as time goes on. Dealing with other people and having to bear the enormity of the interactions can be energy-sapping, and this presents a critical problem for introverts.

There are a number of solutions that you can observe in order to go about the challenges you experience at these events:

Practice giving speeches: This is good advice for anyone who has stage fright because you will be in a position to communicate to a large group of people without making any errors. More importantly, you will have overcome your nervousness as a result of the practice, and this will be instrumental in your mastery of social skills. The practice will also help you prepare to give an appropriate message so that you can overcome a critical problem you experience at social gatherings.

Avoid bringing up work-related issues at the party: There is no point bringing office affairs to the party, even though it is a corporate event. The aim of the party or gathering is to get people to interact, honor hardworking individuals, and create a sense of positivity among everybody else. It is important to keep up the spirit by having interesting conversations and ensuring everybody is as comfortable as possible. Office issues will only kill the momentum of the party.

Appreciate small talk: You must appreciate the essence of small talk as it is the most effective way for people to interact. Small talk allows individuals to bond because you can observe more about their character traits and behavior from the way they talk. These conversations are the life of the event or the party because everybody wants to be casual and speak freely. If you appreciate this as well, then you're on the way to mastering social skills, and you will be able to have many more friends as a result.

See it as an opportunity to make new friends: You must appreciate the party because you are not going to have too many chances to meet people of great diversity. A party allows you to meet many different personalities, and this can be a good opportunity to make friends and learn about new cultures. You need to develop a different perspective about parties because you can easily change your life by meeting new, interesting people. This will enable you to see more meaning from such events, and you will come to appreciate the essence of such social gatherings as they directly contribute to the improvement of your social skills.

Have a drink, try to relax: The most direct way of running away from the challenges of having to interact at a social gathering is to get into the mood. After all, if you cannot beat them, join them. You can easily find yourself having a good time if you keep to yourself but have a drink and try to enjoy some aspect of the party. It is very likely that others will join you, and this will improve the spirit of the gathering, and it will make you appreciate the people around you even more.

Enjoy the music/dance/be lively: Get on the dance floor and move about even if you do not know how to dance. Try and release yourself into the moment because it will help you understand the people around you a little better. It is not necessary for you to be a professional dancer to have a good time because the event is all about releasing that stress and trying to have a good time. Be lively and walk around because this will ensure that you do not get bored. Do not remain fixed in one place at a party because you will not enjoy the real reason for being there.

Link up with people of common interest: While walking about, it is possible to eavesdrop on loud conversations with people who have similar interests. Hang out with them because they will make the event much more fun for you. Listen to what they have to say and contribute to the conversation as this will be an excellent chance to interact. Hanging out with people of shared interests will be a significant boost to your social skills, and it will help make things livelier for you.

Leave early: If you are really not enjoying the party or event, then forcing yourself to be there is not going to help. There are no social skills that you will learn if you are desperately bored and disinterested. The best thing for you is to leave early, but try to prepare for the next gathering by familiarizing yourself with the basic concepts of social skills. At the end of the day, patience will play a big role in your mastery of social skills, and forcing yourself to be a part of larger groups of people will not help.

Chapter 15: Emotional Intelligence

Emotional intelligence refers to the ability to learn and manage personal emotions as well as those of others. It is a way of controlling the way you feel and handling your feelings for other people in society. Handling your emotions is extremely important as it takes you a significant step forward towards understanding yourself. People who have emotional control have better mental health and can interact much better with others in the community. However, it is important to distinguish between emotional quotient (EQ) and intelligence quotient (IQ).

Definition: Whereas emotional intelligence refers to the ability to manage one's own emotions as well as of others, intelligence quotient refers to the result of a standardized intelligence test that shows a person's capability for logical reasoning. There is a clear difference between the two because one handles with emotional control and the other deals with the level of intelligence of a person. Emotional control involves important decisions regarding how a person relates to themselves and the people around them.

Intelligence quotient, however, is the result of an academic endeavor where a statistic is worked out to determine the logical capability of the person.

Ability: Emotional quotient helps a person to identify and express their emotions in society to ensure effective communication. Controlling emotions also means understanding those of the people around you, and this is an important aspect of mastering good social skills. This is different from the intelligence quotient that involves learning to implement knowledge that has been acquired over time. The intelligence quotient shows the ability of a person to retain knowledge over a definite period and how developed their logical and abstract thinking is.

Recognition: Emotional quotient provides recognition to almost anybody in the community with emotional challenges to understand them and learn to deal with them. This is an essential aspect of this factor because it can affect anybody in society. This is a stark difference to the intelligence quotient that identifies only those who excel in the standardized tests. This type of test helps to understand people with mental challenges as well as those with high intellect in the community. Therefore, both tests help to recognize different sets of problems and each aim at tackling the challenges they represent.

Guarantees: Learning to control our emotions by understanding the implications of the emotional quotient enables the individual to achieve success in life. This is because they can focus their emotions on productive endeavors to guarantee success in their efforts in life. This is an important aspect of emotional intelligence because it shows the individual's ability to be in control of themselves. This is a stark difference to the intelligence quotient that helps in understanding somebody's knowledge to guarantee success in school. The intelligence quotient focuses on somebody's ability to learn as opposed to their emotions, and it highlights how best they absorb and retain information over a period of time.

Measures: The emotional quotient provides a measure of how robust a person's emotions are and their ability to control the emotions of others. This means that it assesses the level of happiness and sadness, for example, of the individual and determines how much in control they are and of the people around them. This is different from the intelligence quotient that provides a measure of how intelligent the individual is. From this measurement, it is possible to determine just how smart a person is and how much they have learned and are willing to improve.

Acquisition: Emotional intelligence is something that is learned through time, and it is highly dependent on a person's social skills. Mastery of social skills allows a person to develop emotional intelligence, and this allows them to live a much healthier life in light of all the challenges that exist. As for the intelligence quotient, it is acquired at birth where everybody is born with different levels of intelligence. This is an important difference between the two because one can easily be altered by understanding the importance of social skills while the other is an inborn ability.

What is the importance of emotional intelligence, particularly for you?

It enables a person to have a better understanding of themselves: Emotional intelligence reveals to a person their weaknesses and allows them to improve on these. It is possible to understand what makes a person sad most of the time and develop a mechanism to avoid such emotional problems. Understanding yourself better is a key aspect of mastering social skills as it reveals dark inner secrets about you that you might not want to confront. Similarly, you are in a better position to interact with others as a result of understanding their emotional state.

Learning how to control emotions: Another important aspect of mastering social skills is being able to control emotions and ensuring they do not get out of control. It is possible to spot people who remain very cool, even in sad circumstances such as a funeral without breaking a sweat. Such people have control over their emotions, and it is something they have to learn over time in order to remain composed and understanding. Emotional intelligence allows you not only to control your emotions but also those of the people around you.

To understand others: When you get a better perspective of how emotions affect our lives, it becomes easier to relate to and understand other people. In this instance, emotional intelligence offers a brief moment where you can look into another person's weaknesses and better relate with them. Controlling the emotions of other people can be a tremendous help to both parties because you can help each other avoid different problems associated with emotional control. It becomes much easier and straightforward to deal with people because you develop a better understanding of their preferences and their ability to remain cool in different types of situations.

To cope with pressure and make better decisions: Having emotional intelligence also helps you get around difficult times by providing you with the mental control you require. It becomes a straightforward process handling different pressures of life, and it becomes possible to understand how to motivate yourself. Emotional intelligence, therefore, allows for better decision making because it becomes much easier to control sadness and happiness. The same applies to your friends because you are also in control of their emotions and thus able to guarantee a favorable state of mind. Coping with pressure in life is a sign that you are mastering social skills and are thus able to interact successfully with other people.

There are a number of approaches that can be relied on to improve emotional intelligence and guarantee a much happier life:

Reading up about the concepts: One of the best ways of adding to your knowledge of emotional control is reading up about it and mastering the technical terms. Several online sources will give you appropriate information for learning about emotional control and the measures you can take in your life. Finding out the information for yourself is extremely important in determining success because it provides an inner understanding of the basic concepts of emotions. Reading up online will enable you to come across several works by psychologists on the subject that will give you proper insight into the best approaches for emotional control.

Soliciting friendly help: The assistance of a friend in the process of controlling emotions is invaluable as they will offer practical advice based on what they know about you and their own knowledge. Friendly help will give you a chance to practice your emotions without things getting out of hand, and this will be an effective way of developing your emotional intelligence.

Learning more about social skills: This is an excellent opportunity for you to understand how to apply different types of social skills in different situations in your life. Emotional control enables you to get a better picture of how to apply social skills to control not only your moods but that of the people around you. The importance of social skills becomes more important as you control your emotions because they are responsible for how you present yourself in the community. Getting more information on social skills will enable you to interact successfully with everybody else.

Handling emotions: The most important aspect of mastering emotional intelligence is that it opens the doors towards handling your emotions. You understand the power of sadness and happiness at the same time and how best to apply them to improve your mood and others. Emotional intelligence is linked to mental health because it is about finding the most appropriate way of living with yourself and achieving maximum happiness. If it is possible to guarantee your happiness, then you are in a position to influence the lives of other people around you positively.

Before concluding the chapter, it is important to understand what empathy is. It is an important aspect of emotional intelligence because it refers to the ability to share and comprehend the feelings of another person. Empathy is an important aspect of mastering social skills because it shows an understanding for the people around you and your willingness to help. Taking into consideration how others are feeling can also improve your emotions because there is a positive impact on your emotional control when you make other people happy. Having empathy places you in the shoes of another individual and enables you to have a proper understanding of what they are going through.

Chapter 16: Practical Communication Tips (Additional Tips)

The following list provides helpful communication tips that can assist you in socializing with other people in different circumstances:

Conversation starters: There are many approaches to starting a conversation with a stranger, and the setting of the place is just as important. If you are trying to woo a mate, how you start a conversation will determine whether you will make friends with them. Approaching them with an interesting comment about where you are is a good way of beginning as this will provide you with the attention you need. For instance, if you are at a wedding and you see a beautiful person, you can approach them by commenting on how beautiful the wedding is and how much you like the cake. Conversation starters are also important in a professional setting because they break the ice and allow you to interact with somebody new. Approaching a person by way of small talk is an excellent way of tackling this as it will give you a chance to introduce yourself and your topic of discussion.

How to speak clearly and confidently: There are a number of approaches you can utilize to ensure that you are audible and confident when you communicate with other people. One thing that helps increase confidence as you interact with other people is expressing yourself via your body language and facial expressions. When it is possible to appropriately match your body language with what you are speaking about, you can communicate your message clearly. Many people take body language very seriously, and most of them use it as a basis for communicating and understanding other people. How you present yourself and communicate with your body will determine the clarity of your message. For instance, when presenting a new product to prospective customers, using body language to provide emphasis ensures the clarity of the message you are communicating. If you can achieve this, you end up being more confident because you are approaching the problem of communication with precision. Confidence is created by your ability to be effective at your communication, and this can be furthered by gauging the emotional state of everybody. Match what you are saying to them with the tone in the room; do not communicate excitedly among people who are somber and the opposite is true.

How to stop shyness: There are a number of approaches that can be used to help stop shyness when interacting with other people. First, speaking eloquently on a topic you are interested in helps to get rid of shyness because you can focus on something you know and provide much more information about it. Being knowledgeable about a subject allows you to speak frankly about it without feeling weird in any way or being intimidated by any of the listeners. Another way of avoiding shyness is by maintaining a good mood because it allows you to laugh and engage with other people. Being in a good mood can make you easily forget that you are among several people, and this is an effective way of relaxing and enjoying the company of other people. Shyness can also be avoided by constant practice over time, particularly with the help of a person. Shyness is an indication of inexperience in social circles, and getting to spend more time with other people makes you get used to them. This prevents shyness from becoming a serious problem because you familiarize yourself in front of other people and thus become familiar with how to conduct yourself.

Make people like you immediately: Another important aspect of socializing is getting people to like you instantly as this makes it easy to socialize and enables you to be accepted in their circles. As always, somebody with something interesting to talk about will be instantly liked because they have interesting information to share with the rest of the group. Appreciating the essence of small talk will enable you to come up with intriguing things to talk about, and all attention will be on you because you happen to know exactly what to say. People will also like you immediately if you display the basic tenets of good social skills, such as politeness and empathy. Somebody who is considerate and respectful will easily be liked because they can conduct themselves very well around other people. It is also a good idea to be inquisitive when the situation permits because other people like answering questions, particularly when it applies to them. Understand the type of people that you are around because an inquisitive nature will endear you to one of them and you can interact on that basis.

How to make friends: The most straightforward way of making friends is by being respectful and considerate of other people. In an event or even a professional setting, it is extremely important to be patient and courteous as you interact with other people because a good nature quickly attracts people of a similar nature. Be casual at the same time as interested in the people you are with because a positive attitude will make them like you within a short period, and you will be able to make friends and have fun. Always have something interesting to talk about as this is the main aspect of the interaction between two people. Your intelligence can play a big role in securing friendship because you can pursue topics of similar interest with the respective individual. Find common ground with a colleague and focus on discussing specific subjects; over time, you will be able to make friends with them because there will always be a chance of regular communication. Successful interactions are responsible for making new friends, and this becomes even more important by understanding the basics of having good social skills in society.

How to talk to anyone with confidence: Confidence is something that you can gain over time through practice, and it is important also to have a courageous spirit. Confidence cannot be acquired if you are weak at heart because it requires you to interact with others wholesomely and understand their emotions. Comprehending the art of speech giving, for example, is critical to developing confidence because the basic lessons earned in this endeavor help create confidence in a person. Somebody must be brave and willing to stand in front of other people without feeling any form of intimidation, and it is possible to achieve this by mastering social skills. Preparation is everything when you want to talk with confidence because you can organize your thoughts systematically. Planning ahead gives you a chance to find out difficult aspects of what you want to talk about, and arming yourself with this knowledge is pivotal in ensuring your confidence is there. Confidence can also be acquired by understanding the emotional state of the person you are speaking to, which will give a better perspective on their state of mind. This way, you can speak without fear of offending them, and you build your confidence more as you understand their character and traits.

How to charm anyone: One of the most important aspects of being charming is the ability to be knowledgeable in what you want to discuss as well as having good social skills to communicate. A charming person is always intelligent and can discuss almost anything without any fear. Shyness is not something you will find on a charming person because they can give themselves confidence when they interact with other people. Being knowledgeable on a specific subject and maintaining it as the topic of conversation will guarantee that you are charming because you are talking about something interesting. Maintain the concentration of the other person by sticking to a subject you are good at, and this will make them like you immediately. Being charming is also about being respectful to the person you are communicating with and making them feel as comfortable as possible with you. Everybody likes another person who treats them with careful regard and understanding of their likes.

Communication skills (general): Communication skills can be learned over time, and the key to success is to improve on your ability to communicate. The first step is understanding the basics, such as body language and facial expressions as they form an important basis for successful communication. Learning to communicate with ordinary bodily cues greatly improves communication skills because it is possible to reach out to a large number of people. Communication skills can always be improved through practice, and asking a friend to help in this situation can be a good idea. Try out different communication techniques, learning to understand their differences depending on the different situations that they are applicable. Achieving success in social skills means that the mastery of good communication skills is inevitable. This will allow you to speak to people of different personalities and enable you to diversify your friends. Communication skills can also be learned by observing the way other people communicate, particularly extroverts as they have a natural appeal interacting with others. Emulating the way extrovert people interact and communicate with other people will give you an insight into how to develop your communication skills.

Chapter 17: Inspiring Individuals

Introverts have much to learn from leaders of the world and celebrity figures on the most effective ways of acquiring social skills. Emulating the example set by well-known characters can be of significant help in understanding how to interact with others. A good majority of the people who make the headlines are usually extroverts, and the example they set can be a useful guide on developing social skills in society. Several extrovert people get their inspiration from such figures, and the same can be applied for introverts looking to boost their social skills. The following is a list of well-known individuals that can offer you an example on how to interact in society:

Donald Trump: The character of the President of the United States offers an example of how leaders speak and exercise their social skills. The president is open and brash when addressing the public, and he manages to maintain the concentration of the people by being outgoing and fearless. This is an important trait for you to learn because it shows a standard way of gaining the attention of everybody else and maintaining it. However, it is necessary to learn the importance of being humble by watching any fiery Trump speech.

Keanu Reeves: The famous actor is the opposite of Trump and displays a very reserved personality both on the screen and in real life. The actor shows that it is not a must for you to be excessively loud and brash if you want to communicate effectively. Being confident in yourself is just as important a trait like any other, and it is responsible for keeping the attention of your listeners. One can focus on speaking more sense than being very loud, and this will be instrumental in successfully interacting with other people.

Barack Obama: This is a character that is very much loved by everybody else, and this is because of the intelligence he displays while speaking. One thing we can learn from Obama is that preparing yourself before addressing other people is extremely important. It makes all the difference in what you are going to say and how you will deliver this message. Approaching interactions with other people by relying on intelligent appeal keeps up their concentration and enables them to like you even more. The main take from Obama is that you can also be humble and respectful, but be mindful of what you say to other people.

Theresa May: The British Prime Minister is also a quiet talker but very effective in getting her points across. This is because she speaks firmly and with confidence whenever she is presenting her points, and her stone-faced approach to handling issues should be an inspiration for an introvert. Observe how she handles the media because she demands respect subtly by presenting herself appropriately. Be firm and unwavering in the way you present your information, and you will find it easy to interact with like-minded people.

Pope Francis: The Pope is a humble and even shy individual and speaks quietly even when addressing a multitude of people. This is an important trait to observe in the head of the Catholic Church because it shows there is no need to be loud and brash. Approaching a conversation with good grace and humility endears the people around you, and they will offer you an opportunity to speak as a result. The lesson that can be learned from the Pope is that silence is not a bad thing when interacting because it is better to be composed than to expose your ignorance by being too loud.

Oprah Winfrey: This is an open person who likes to talk freely and fearlessly with her audience. Her communication technique is reliant on providing lots of information, body language and consideration for the language that she speaks. Oprah is a good example of the importance of confidence when communicating, and her social skills have been developed based on this trait. The importance of being open-minded is evident when listening to Oprah and it is possible to learn a great deal about social skills by looking at how she interacts with her audience.

Vladimir Putin: The President of the Russian Federation is a firm talker, and he provides inspiration on how to interact with others. Putin shows a unique way of communicating because he rarely incorporates body language and facial gestures but still manages to come across clearly. The clarity of the message being communicated is important as is confidence and firmness. Putin always prepares for his press conferences, and even when he responds to questions, there is a sense of preparation with the meticulousness he gives to every response. He shows that it is possible to minimize other forms of bodily communication yet be very effective when reaching out to other people.

Beyoncé: This is a well-known celebrity who has built her reputation on producing good music. Her communication style is based on several things, from her dressing to the calmness of her voice. She always insists on addressing each person individually, and she has a general demeanor for when she performs on stage. The lesson we can learn from this celebrity is that presentation plays an essential role in how we communicate. Your social skills are likely to be enhanced if you can present yourself before others ostentatiously to keep their attention.

Melania Trump: This is another silent speaker, and she displays the signs of an extrovert by how she remains withdrawn. She speaks very gently and shows the necessity of having information beforehand whenever addressing other people. There is no need to be excessively brash because it is still possible to get a message across even by remaining calm and composed. It is better to draw the respect of others by maintaining your cool rather than attempting something big and ending up not communicating effectively.

Conclusion

Thank you for making it through to the end of *Social Skills: How to Analyze People and Body Language Instantly, Handle Small Talk and Conversation as an Introvert, Improve Emotional Intelligence, and Learn Highly Effective Communication Tips*. It should have been informative and provided you with all of the tools you need to achieve your goals.

The information provided in this book offered guidance on the best ways that an introvert can socialize with other people in society and fit in comfortably. This is because introverts tend to be withdrawn, and many people assume that they lack the social skills to enable them to display extrovert behaviors. The first sections of this book provided information about introvert traits and how to deal with social anxiety. Practical advice was given on how to set objectives in order to improve social skills and allow introverts to be in a position to interact with others successfully.

The book emphasized the importance of maintaining good social skills as this is the key to successfully fitting into society. The book also provided information on the best ways of analyzing people, and there was much information about body language and facial expressions. There was also a discussion of the different personality traits as well as the best approaches for introverts to interact with other people. The focus was on the challenges that introverts face, and there was even a discussion on small talk and how to conduct it successfully. The book further described how to interact at social events and gave practical advice on social skills in such situations, as well as a discussion about emotional intelligence – an important factor to consider when understanding how to deal with other people.

The book rounded off by providing practical communication tips and listing some popular figures to provide inspiration for learning social skills.

The next step is to go forth and start utilizing the tips, tricks, tools, and techniques provided in this book to begin realizing your social skills potential and become confident and empowered as your journey into the world of social skills improvement progresses.

Don't judge yourself if your progress is slow at first – just stick with it, and you'll see how much you can achieve. Moreover, there are likely to be techniques that come more naturally to you than others, so don't worry – it evens out, and you will become more confident with your social skills the more you practice.

Finally, if you found this book useful in any way, a review on Amazon is always appreciated!

Here's another book by Matt Holden that you might like

Made in the USA
Middletown, DE
14 December 2020